MW01098721

QUICK BRIGHT THINGS

QUICK BRIGHT THINGS

A PLAY BY CHRISTOPHER COOK

PLAYWRIGHTS CANADA PRESS
TORONTO

LIBRARY AND ARCHIVES CANADA CATALOGUING IN PUBLICATION
Title: Quick bright things / a play by Christopher Cook.
Names: Cook, Christopher, 1983- author.
Description: First edition.
Identifiers: Canadiana (print) 20200189085 | Canadiana (ebook) 20200189107 | ISBN 9780369100863 (softcover) | ISBN 9780369100870 (PDF) | ISBN 9780369100887 (EPUB) | ISBN 9780369100894 (Kindle)
Classification: LCC PS8605.O625 Q53 2020 | DDC C812/.6—dc23

Playwrights Canada Press operates on Mississaugas of the Credit, Wendat, Anishinaabe, Métis, and Haudenosaunee land. It always was and always will be Indigenous land.

We acknowledge the financial support of the Canada Council for the Arts—which last year invested $153 million to bring the arts to Canadians throughout the country—the Ontario Arts Council (OAC), Ontario Creates, and the Government of Canada for our publishing activities.

Canada Council
for the Arts

Conseil des arts
du Canada

ONTARIO ARTS COUNCIL
CONSEIL DES ARTS DE L'ONTARIO

an Ontario government agency
un organisme du gouvernement de l'Ontario

ONTARIO CREATES | ONTARIO CRÉATIF

For Scott Button.

The researcher Kathleen Montague discovered dopamine in 1957. You were born decades later, and the destiny of my dopamine firing was ordained.

INTRODUCTION

I wrote the first scene of *Quick Bright Things* more than ten years ago, soon after I completed a program for emerging playwrights and just before I enrolled in my first undergraduate psychology course. For the next few years, I was too terrified to write the rest of the play—the characters, the story, and the subject of mental wellness all intimidated me to such an extent that I shelved the script.

Now, ten years on, I've taken a few more psychology courses—in fact, after completing a graduate degree, I work as a therapist in private practice—and mental wellness is a subject I often return to as a playwright.

Conversations about mental health can still be so hard. Imagine telling a new friend that you see a therapist. Why might that give us pause? Why does it feel like coming out of the mental health closet? The way we talk about wellness in our communities has grown by leaps and bounds in the last few decades. But fear, discomfort, confusion, and prejudice remain, so we must keep leaping.

As a kid, like a couple of the characters in the play, I could give you a plot summary of every single *Star Trek: The Next Generation* episode. I loved science fiction. It was a different way of perceiving, of knowing the world. There is an incredible number of ways of knowing in this world. Some, like sci-fi, fall into what we call (relatively) "normal." Others don't. We must keep leaping.

Quick Bright Things deals with mental wellness, and it's also a play about family and the ways that we love each other.

Ready to leap?

Christopher Cook
Vancouver, 2020

NOTES

The text is meant to be delivered quickly. Don't be polite—step on each other's lines and talk over one another.

Although Gerome was recently diagnosed with schizophrenia, he has probably been managing symptoms on his own, without medical support, for years. Similarly, his parents, Nick and Toby, have likely been managing their son's symptoms in different ways without realizing it.

The symptoms associated with a schizophrenia diagnosis can take many different forms and vary across individuals. Gerome is one character in a play in which all of the characters are on mental wellness journeys of one kind or another. Their journeys are uniquely their own and are not generalizable.

Quick Bright Things was developed through Delinquent Theatre's Playwrights in Residence Program and presented as part of their Write Minds festival at Progress Lab 1422, Vancouver, in March 2014, with the following cast and creative team:

Gerome: Matt Reznek
Nick: Marcus Youssef
Marion: Dawn Petten
Reid: Andrew McNee
Michael: Amitai Marmorstein
Saski: Julie McIsaac

Director: Laura McLean
Dramaturge: Christine Quintana

Quick Bright Things was first produced by Persephone Theatre, Saskatoon, in October 2017, with the following cast and creative team:

Gerome: Jordan Harvey
Nick: Rick Hughes
Marion: Anita Smith
Reid: Aaron Hursh
Michael: Samuel DeGirolamo
Saski: Heather Morrison

Director: Del Surjik
Production Dramaturge: Johnna Wright
Set Designer: Ross Nichol
Costume Designer: Terri Bauer
Lighting Designer: Byron Hnatuk
Sound Designer: Gilles Zolty
Assistant Director: Jaron Francis
Stage Manager: Jennifer Rathie-Wright
Assistant Stage Manager: Robert Grier

And ere a man hath power to say, "Behold!"
The jaws of darkness do devour it up:
So quick bright things come to confusion.
—Shakespeare, *A Midsummer Night's Dream*

I'm fighting normal. I'm choreographing
this other dance, where you spin across
the floor and out the door while the other
kids are still jumping on the spot
—Brad Cran, "Normal"

The New York State Mental Hygiene Department reported yesterday that new chemical agents might revolutionize the treatment of both mild and serious mental afflictions.
—Robert K. Plumb, "Drug Use Hailed in Mental Cases,"
New York Times, October 7, 1955

All psychiatric treatments cause brain dysfunction ... brain-disability is the primary "therapeutic" effect, and ... cases are seen as successful when this impairment is interpreted as an improvement. The principle applies to lobotomy, electroshock and all psychiatric medications.
—Peter R. Breggin, "Intoxication Anosognosia:
The Spellbinding Effect of Psychiatric Drugs,"
International Journal of Risk and Safety in Medicine, 2007

Antipsychotic drugs can be regarded as implements of social control, but they can also help individuals gain relief from intense and intrusive psychiatric experiences ... Sometimes, when people are locked into an internal reality they cannot escape, this chemical suppression can bring them back into contact with the real world, and ... re-establish relations with other people. These benefits come at a price, however.
—Joanna Moncrieff, *The Bitterest Pills:*
The Troubling Story of Antipsychotic Drugs, 2013

CHARACTERS

Gerome: A seventeen-year-old.
Nick: Gerome's adoptive father, late forties.
Marion: Gerome's aunt, late thirties.
Reid: Gerome's uncle, early fifties.
Michael: Gerome's cousin, thirteen.
Saski: Gerome's biological mother, early thirties.

SCENE

The place is Thunder Bay, Ontario. The principal setting is the open living room/dining room area of Reid and Marion's home. Scene One begins and ends outside the house; Scene Two takes place in the bathroom; Scene Three ends in a car; Scene Five is in the woods. Of course, these settings may be represented realistically, but they need not be.

Props mentioned in the stage directions and dialogue may prove useful, but, again, liberties may be taken in terms of representation.

TIME

The action occurs over one weekend, from Friday night to Sunday afternoon.

SCENE ONE

Friday night. NICK and GEROME stand facing us downstage. They are outside of MARION and REID's home. The open living room/dining room area of REID and MARION's house is dimly lit behind them. NICK wears shorts and boat shoes; GEROME wears a worn-looking tie and suit jacket. GEROME is a little too big for his clothes. GEROME is noticeably anxious.

NICK: . . . Ready?

GEROME shakes his head.

Two hours. Tops. Eat and run.

NICK adjusts GEROME's tie.

Then it's you, me, and the wilds of Ontario for the rest of the weekend.

GEROME: And her.

NICK: Yeah, and her. For sure. Well I'm feeling ready.

GEROME: Ha.

NICK: I am! I'm ready. I'm just gonna text your dad and let him know we arrived.

NICK does. GEROME watches him. NICK looks up. He smiles at his son.

You look good.

NICK takes a selfie with his son—GEROME makes a "weird" face at the last moment—and then NICK sends the text. GEROME takes off his tie and puts it over his papa's head.

Whoa whoa whoa—

GEROME gives him a look.

GEROME: Papa.

NICK lets GEROME tighten the tie around his neck. NICK's cellphone rings.

NICK: Now your dad's calling me. You wanna talk?

GEROME shakes his head.

Me neither.

NICK silences the phone and looks down at the tie.

Okay. We all set?

GEROME nods. NICK loosens the tie. A shift as NICK knocks and MARION enters.

MARION: I'MCOMINGI'MCOMINGI'MCOMING!

MARION opens the door and hugs NICK.

There you two are! Could you have called?

NICK: Yep. Could've. Pretty busy driving the last day and a half.

MARION: *(calling off)* REID, THEY'RE ACTUALLY HERE!

Every time MARION—*or anyone else—yells,* NICK *and* GEROME *both brace themselves.*

NICK: How are ya, Marion?

MARION: Me? Don't worry about me. How are you and—heeeey, Geromey.

GEROME: *(quietly)* Hi.

MARION *waves at him.*

MARION: How ya feeling? Don't be shy. It's Auntie Marion.

NICK: He knows who you are.

MARION: Of course he does—

MARION *gives* GEROME *a big hug.* GEROME *doesn't hug back.*

Look, Geromey—*une, deux, trois,* right to the bone—*trois* nails stressing whether you two were dead on the highway or ditched us or I dunno what, but I blame your papa.

NICK *offers up a bottle of wine.*

NICK: How about a bottle of wine to make up for it?

MARION: Oh jeez, Nick—actually no—you are now entering an Alky Free Zone—

(calling off) REID! COME SAY HELLO TO YOUR BROTHER!

NICK: A what?

MARION: Alky. Free. Zone. I'm not letting you cross this threshold till you ditch the booze.

NICK: It's a Riesling. "Booze" seems a little derogatory—

MARION: I've never known alcohol to get offended.

NICK: It's a hostess gift.

MARION: That is so sweet—it's the thought that counts—

NICK: And the thirty-five dollars—

MARION: And we appreciate the thought, so leave it on the porch—yep right there—you can pick it up on your way out.

NICK and GEROME move into the living room/dining room area of REID and MARION's home—comfortably upper middle class.

Now welcome—

(calling off) REID, WHERE THE HECK—

REID enters from the kitchen.

REID: Gerome. My man. Looking sharp.

GEROME smiles.

Nicky. Asshole. Thanks for showing up. I'm fucking starving.

MARION: Michael had to eat—he couldn't wait.

NICK: That's fine.

MARION: I'll still make him sit with us—

(calling off) MICHAEL!

REID tugs on NICK's tie.

REID: This thing's making me wanna poke my eyes out.

NICK: It's Gerome's actually.

REID: Must be your face I'm reacting to. Where's Toby? He's what I like best about you.

NICK: Couldn't take time off work—

MARION: Uh-oh, one dad's missing. It's not a real family vacation!

MARION sits down at the table and NICK and REID join her. NICK sits between REID and MARION. GEROME hangs back from the table.

(calling off) EARTH TO MICHAEL, PLEASE! GET DOWN HERE!

NICK: *(to GEROME)* You wanna go wash your hands? You didn't forget, I'm just reminding you.

GEROME exits quickly. REID and MARION watch him.

He's real serious. About cleanliness.

MARION: Good. Good! Does he need help?

NICK: Washing his hands?

(to REID) I don't know how long we can stay.

REID: Missed you too, broski.

NICK: We still gotta get to the campsite and set up the tent—

MARION: When we heard you were camping, we laughed soooo hard.

MARION and REID crack up at the thought.

NICK: Yeah. *(re: food)* This looks really—

REID: *(re: food)* Pretty fucking nice, eh?

NICK: Thank you for having us, Marion—

REID: *(re: food)* You know what that is, Nicky boy?

MARION: Are you kidding? Finally pulled you away from *Montréal*—

REID: That right there, Nicksters—

MARION: About time for a Thunder Bay pick-me-up!

REID: —is one big-ass roast beast!

NICK: I know what it is, Reid. But I forgot to tell you—Gerome's gone vegan.

MARION: No, you didn't tell us that at all—

NICK: It's a new thing—not a big a deal—

REID: Naw, no biggie—we got chicken—Marion'll cook him up some chick-chick.

NICK: He's vegan.

REID: He eats chicken.

NICK: VEGAN.

MARION: All right, we might all have different definitions of the term *vaygen—*

(calling off) MICHAEL, I AM COUNTING TO THREE—ONE . . .

REID: *(calling off)* GEROME! WHAT'D YOU WANT, MY MAN? WANT SOME CHICK-CHICK?

MARION: There's broccoli, will he eat broccoli?

(calling off) TWO!

NICK: Yep, that's great—

MARION: TWO AND A HALF . . . LAST WARNING, YOUNG MAN!

MICHAEL enters from upstairs with headphones on.

MICHAEL: Hey, Reeeeon, how about we practise our inside voice?

MARION gives MICHAEL a hug.

MARION: Squishes—you missed the hugs!

MICHAEL pushes her away.

MICHAEL: We'd like you better if you weren't so friggin' crazy.

MARION: Oooh-kay uh-uh—remember what we talked about.

REID yanks off MICHAEL's headphones and gestures to NICK.

MICHAEL: Hi, Uncle N.

NICK: Hey, Mike.

GEROME enters and keeps his distance from the table. Throughout the following, NICK will try to keep checking in with his son. GEROME mostly ignores him.

MARION: And your cousin—say "hi" to Geromey.

MICHAEL gives him a single wave. REID flicks him.

MICHAEL: Ow! Dad! What's your problem?

REID gestures to GEROME.

MICHAEL makes an exaggerated wave at GEROME.

HELLO!

GEROME gives MICHAEL the Vulcan "live long and prosper" salute. MICHAEL snickers at him. Pause.

REID: Oh well done, boys. Don't spend yourselves all at once—save it for the Get-To-Know-You-Better-slash-Catch-Up-Shit we got planned for later tonight . . . Talk to each other!

MARION: *(to GEROME)* What's wrong? You're being so quiet!

MARION tries to mouth the words "can he speak?" to NICK, pointing at GEROME.

NICK: What?

MARION tries to whisper—unsuccessfully.

MARION: Can he speak?

NICK: Of course—

GEROME: *(blurting, nervously)* I AM HAPPY TO BE HERE EATING WITH YOU ALL.

MICHAEL laughs. GEROME joins in.

MARION: There he is!

(to NICK) I thought maybe that was a symptom.

NICK: Nope. He's just taking you all in.

MARION gestures for GEROME to sit down. He does, sitting between MARION and MICHAEL. NICK is caught between REID and MARION, and GEROME is caught between MICHAEL and MARION for the rest of the meal.

REID: So is anyone partaking in the fucking roast beast now?

MARION: Babe, please! We have a *vaygen* present.

GEROME holds out his plate.

REID: Lookie here—our wimpy-ass veggie's first in line—

MARION: *(to NICK)* Holding out his plate like that—what is that? What does it mean?

REID: Gee I dunno, Marion—seems like pretty universal fucking English for "load me up some BEAST"!

REID & MICHAEL: *(chanting)* LOAD UP THE BEAST! LOAD UP THE BEAST! LOAD UP THE BEAST!

NICK: *(to GEROME)* You really want some?

REID: Lay off—we're curing him the ol' fashioned way. Who's next?

MARION: What would people like to drink? We've got water and—ah—more water!

MICHAEL: Pop! Can I have pop?

MARION: Um, not on the menu—

(to NICK) We're on a cleanse: eat everything, but you only get water.

(to MICHAEL) Meaning no soda pop.

MICHAEL: Dad, I get all the caffeine I want at Mom's house.

REID: So go back to your mom's house.

MARION: *(to REID)* Drinks—? Can you—?

REID: What's everybody having again? Oh yeah—round of water on the house.

> REID *exits to the kitchen.* NICK *tries to make eye contact with* GEROME, *who is still ignoring him.*

MARION: Your brother and I missed you soooo much—

(calling off) RIGHT, REID?

REID: *(off)* WHAT?

MARION: And see—how hard is it to stop in for dinner and a catch-up?

NICK: It's a nineteen-and-a-half-hour drive.

MARION: And a three-hour flight—give us a little more warning, we'll buy you tickets.

NICK: Will do.

> *NICK is giving GEROME an inquisitive "thumbs up," trying to get him to respond. MARION responds instead with two big thumbs up at NICK.*

(to GEROME) Bud? Okay?

> *GEROME nods.*

> *Pause. The sound of cutlery on plates.*

MARION: *(to NICK)* What are you up to right now—still at that restaurant?

NICK: Atomic Cowboy's a club actually—

MICHAEL: You work at a club?

MARION: I *love* that it was cowboys—when I heard that I'm sitting here thinking every night must be like *yee-ha*!

MICHAEL: That's so cool.

NICK: But I'm at home full time now.

MARION: Why didn't you tell us?

(calling off) REID!

MICHAEL: *(to NICK)* How many shots can you do before you puke?

MARION: YOUR BROTHER IS UNEMPLOYED!

NICK: No, actually—

MICHAEL: Did you get super drunk every night?

REID: *(off)* I THOUGHT HE WAS BABYSITTING GEROME!

MICHAEL: Uncle N!

NICK: Yes, Mike?

MARION: *(calling off)* COME ON, REID!

MICHAEL: "Yes," you got super drunk? Did you get fired?

REID: *(off)* WHAT? HE GOT FIRED?

NICK: No!

MARION: *(calling off)* OFFER HIM A DARN JOB!

REID: *(off)* KNOW ANYTHING ABOUT PRIVATE SECURITY, NICKY?

MARION: *(calling off)* TEACH HIM!

(to NICK) We'd love you to come work for us.

NICK: Thank you, I don't need—

MARION: No standing on ceremony. We're the second-largest private security solutions provider in northwestern Ontario, and we gotta be generous—we gotta hire family.

NICK: Be a hell of a commute every morning.

MARION: Where's the gun to your head saying you can't move back to the Thunder Dome?

NICK: I already have a job—

(to GEROME) We already have a job.

REID enters from the kitchen with four glasses of water.

REID: Okay, got a water—that yours? Another water here. And looks like—yep—water, water.

MARION: Where's yours?

REID: I'm saving myself for a better offer.

MICHAEL: Dad! Work in a bar like Uncle N before he got fired and get hammered for free.

REID: *(to NICK)* You're a fucking layabout now?

NICK: I'm home-schooling Gerome.

REID: *(to GEROME)* What's he teaching you?

MICHAEL: *(to NICK)* Have you taught him black holes?

MARION: Michael did a presentation on black holes in science today.

NICK: We haven't done—

GEROME: *(quickly, softly)* Black holes: leftover star bits with gravitational tidal forces strong enough to crush everything while tearing it to nothingness at the same time.

MARION: WOWZERS, THERE'S OUR A+ STUDENT!

MICHAEL: Actually, they're black and they suck up light is the answer. "BLACK hole." Can you do like a backflip?

GEROME shakes his head.

How about a front flip?

GEROME shakes his head.

Gawd, what's wrong with you?

MARION: There's nothing wrong with him, hun. I can't do a backflip either.

MICHAEL: We know you can't Mary-rion. But what's he got?

MARION: Why don't you tell Geromey about gymnastics?

REID: Hey, how 'bout we not call it that? "Gymnastics." He's not hanging out with a bunch of six-year-old girls and doing somersaults.

MARION: *(to NICK)* We signed him up for after-school GYMNASTICS, and he loves it.

REID: Acrobatic Arts! Your nephew—my son—is a competitive gymnast. No joke, this kid—prodigy. You didn't hear it from me cuz I'm biased, but put these words together in your head: Michael Pinel—Pommel Horse Genius—Olympics 2028, Los Angeles. Be there—he's gonna get a gold for his ol' man, I swear to god!

MICHAEL: Can you do a backflip, Uncle N?

NICK: No.

MICHAEL: I can.

GEROME puts his hand up.

MARION: Uh—yes, Geromey?

REID: Look at that plate! Pile of meat—decimated! My man, you're kicking a vegan's ass right now. This is you getting better.

MARION: But save room for dessert—

(announcing) Everyone save room for dessert! We're having pineapple!

REID: No we aren't. Really—again?

MARION: Who doesn't love pineapple? It's full of vitamins and it'll make us fertile.

REID: Watch your language.

MARION: There's nothing wrong with talking about fertilization.

REID: No one wants to be more fertile but you!

MARION: BABE! Why don't we ask Nick and Geromey about their big trip?

NICK: We're doing a papa-son camping trip for the weekend.

GEROME: And meeting my birther.

REID: Your— Oh.

MARION: He means his—

REID: I got it.

MARION: That is so, so—mmm! Yes. You go find her.

REID: Oh Christ.

MARION: And when you do, you shake her hand—because that's what I would do if I met her.

REID: We know you would, babe, but that's retarded.

MARION: LANGUAGE!

NICK: Can we keep our voices down?

MARION: THAT'S FINE. I'M NOT YELLING AND WE'RE NOT USING LANGUAGE LIKE THAT—NOT A NICE WORD!

REID: Says who?

(re: GEROME) He's not retarded. He's wacko.

MARION: CAN WE STOP USING NASTY WORDS!

NICK: Really, Reid? Really?

GEROME *and* MICHAEL *are both laughing at the adults.*

REID: He gets it. We're pissing around.

MARION: *(to GEROME)* Don't listen to him—shake her hand and tell her . . . "hi" from me.

REID: Let's not get him too excited about meeting a lady who—

MARION: SHE'S NOT SOME RANDOM LADY—she's his biological mommy—

NICK: Hang on—"mommy"?

MARION: What else are we gonna call Geromey's—

NICK: Gerome. He doesn't like "Geromey" anymore.

MARION: *(to GEROME)* Oh that's how come I don't exist! Is that why you haven't been answering me?

MARION, trying to be playful, speaks in exaggerated tones.

"QUIT IT WITH THE BABY NAMES, AUNTIE MARION"?

NICK: Can we be cognizant of the tension level? It can affect—

MARION: "Cognizant"?

NICK: It means—

MARION: I know what it means. I just don't think I've ever heard anyone real use it in a sentence. I don't understand who that's—was that directed at me?

NICK: Not you—everyone.

MARION: Excuse me. I'm going to get the salad.

MARION exits to the kitchen. Pause.

REID: *(to MICHAEL, re: GEROME)* Take him outside and play.

MICHAEL: I'll only do it for five cans of pop.

REID: Get the hell outta here, no deal.

MICHAEL: Okay—one can, one can!

REID: Go!

MICHAEL stands up from the table and sizes GEROME up.

MICHAEL: *(to GEROME)* I'll start you off with cartwheels.

GEROME stands to follow MICHAEL out. NICK takes off the tie and goes to put it back on his son, but GEROME grabs the tie and puts it on himself.

NICK: You gonna be okay?

REID: They'll be fine.

GEROME and MICHAEL exit outside.

NICK: *(calling after)* Have fun!

REID: Let's go shooting tomorrow.

NICK: No.

REID: Come on, why not?

NICK: Cuz no.

REID: How you making out right now? You need money?

NICK: Toby got a second job—he's making enough.

REID offers some money. NICK takes it.

REID: But you won't come shooting?

NICK: How's he look to you?

REID: Gerome? . . . Ahhhh. The same basically. He was always weird.

NICK: He's mostly nervous—he just gets anxious sometimes.

REID: What the hell for? It's just us. He knows us.

NICK: Yeah, that's probably why he's anxious.

REID slaps NICK too hard on the back.

REID: That's probably why you're anxious, Nicky boy.

MARION enters from the kitchen with a salad. She's quietly crying.

What the fuck are you doing?

MARION: What does it look like? I'm serving salad.

REID: Quit making those sounds.

MARION: Oh, I'm so sorry, are you getting a little upset too? Well, good, because this is upsetting this whole thing is. Nick, we were reading up online—

NICK: Oh god.

MARION: There's a new drug—look, I printed it out—

(to REID) Where's the paper?

REID: I dunno.

NICK: These are some Dr. Google search results, right?

MARION looks around for the paper.

MARION: You call us up and announce you're showing up for dinner and drop this bomb that our nephew— Reid, I gave it to you! Where is it?

REID: I don't know!

MARION: What medication do they have him on?

NICK: We're exploring different options. How much did you tell Michael?

REID: Are we keeping it hush-hush?

NICK: He's too young to understand. And Gerome's fine.

MARION: We know, but with his, his . . . *phreeeenia.*

NICK: His what?

MARION: His schizo*phreeeenia.* We have to be careful.

NICK: Okay, it's getting pretty late—

MARION: Your beds are all made up. Why go camping when you can visit?

NICK: Because I want to do something normal with my son.

MARION: You're gonna invite his biological mommy over to your tent for marshmallows?

NICK: There's no plan. We haven't even talked to her yet.

MARION: Bring her over here so she can see that his adoptive family is—is—

REID: Fuckin' bitchin'.

MARION: Exactly—flippin' terrific! Come on, do you think camping is healthy in his condition?

NICK: He's in recovery—

REID: What happened? Did he lose it?

NICK: No—he was having trouble.

REID: With what?

NICK: Reality.

REID: I think that's what "losing it" means.

MARION: He was hospitalized?

NICK: A few weeks ago.

MARION: A few weeks ago!

NICK: For a few days!

MARION: Okay, okay, okay. Well, if I were him, I'd want to meet my mommm—ah, my biological parents too. It's genetic.

NICK: They don't know that. They don't know anything.

MARION: But chances are. According to WebMD.

REID holds up the paper.

REID: *(to MARION)* Right in front of your face.

MARION takes the paper.

MARION: The most important thing is to find the right medication, and they've had some real success with this drug. "Patients suffering from schizophrenia . . . show markedly reduced paranoia—hallucinations—"

MARION scans the page.

Oh boy, "side effects"—this one might make him fat—

REID: So the kid's a little chunky—so what the fuck? As long as they uncrazy him, we're fine.

NICK: "Uncrazy him"?

MARION offers NICK the paper.

MARION: Show it to Toby. What's the harm?

NICK: THE HARM IS—

NICK catches himself.

You know how many antipsychotic meds are out there?

REID: Yeah, but this one sounds like the best.

NICK takes the paper.

NICK: He could try a new one every year until he's almost forty and maybe—just maybe—they'll figure out one that works without costing him who he is.

REID: What are you talking about?

NICK: I'm talking about the effects—

REID: Who cares if he's a little chunky! They're just side effects!

NICK: No, listen! They aren't side effects! They're not minor—they're-they're-they're not off to one side, out of view, these are what the drugs DO TO HIM—real effects that are lethal. And it's all guesswork anyway! "Hmmm, what should his dosage be? Let's try two spoonfuls. Nope! That didn't work!" They're wailing on his brain with their fists—nuking him with these pills—and what's the difference? He keeps on getting further from me.

MICHAEL enters from outside.

MICHAEL: Uncle N?

MARION: What is it, hun?

MICHAEL: I don't know where Gerome went.

MARION: What do you mean?

NICK jumps up and the others follow him outside.

NICK: *(calling out)* Gerome!

REID: Which way did he go?

MICHAEL shakes his head.

MICHAEL: I was in the middle of a cartwheel.

MARION: Check all the shrubs! Ninety-nine percent of the time they're in the bushes—that's the first place you look—

REID pulls out an extendable baton and pops it open.

NICK: What are you doing?

REID: Standard procedure.

NICK: This isn't your security detail!

REID: The bushes are prickly!

NICK: Put it away!

(calling out) Gerome! We're leaving now!

MARION: *(calling out)* But you can stay if you want to!

(to NICK) If I were him, I might be hiding because I don't wanna go.

MICHAEL does cartwheels behind them throughout the following.

NICK: He's probably walking into town. I'm gonna circle the block—

REID: I'll drive.

MARION takes out her cell.

MARION: Do we call 911?

NICK: It's under control.

MARION: Excuse me—you don't know if your son is dancing down the middle of the highway or attacking one of our poor neighbours' pets because he's mixed it up with a demon or a furry black hole—and you don't think we need backup?

MICHAEL winds up for another cartwheel.

Michael! You are soooo talented and I love you very very much, but PLEASE stay still.

MICHAEL: Um . . .

They all look to MICHAEL. MICHAEL points up. They look off.

MARION: Oh sweet baby Jay.

NICK: *(calling off)* Bud. No one's mad—

MARION grabs the baton from REID and starts waving it in the air.

MARION: *(calling off)* YOU! DOWN! NOW! That roof is not a playground!

NICK: *(calling off)* Ready to go set up camp?

MARION: *(calling off)* Don't think I can't see that wine bottle! If I see you sip, you are in BIG TROUBLE! I'm calling the fire department.

REID: Stop, stop—watch.

(calling off) I'll give you twenty bucks if you come down here right now.

They wait.

GEROME: *(off)* Michael taught me to do a cartwheel.

MARION: Oh my dear lord, he's having a psychotic attack!

NICK: No, he's all right!

MARION starts climbing onto REID.

MARION: Help me up there—

REID: Get off me!

NICK: We have a system. He says "red alert" in Klingon when he's having trouble. That's our signal.

REID laughs.

REID: No shit?

(to MARION) Babe, my favourite Trekkie ever—he likes *Star Trek* as much as you do! What's "red alert" in Klingon?

MARION: This isn't time for laughing—or *Star Trek*!

REID removes a twenty from his wallet and holds it up. He whistles and waves it in GEROME's direction. They watch as GEROME climbs down.

REID: *(to NICK, quietly)* Bam! What'd I tell you? A little game I like to call Compensation Reinforcement.

GEROME enters with the wine bottle and gives it to MARION. There are big wet blotches on his pants.

MICHAEL: He peed himself.

MARION: A little pee's okay—we're happy you're down safe.

REID: Come on, it's gross. You still get twenty bucks but . . . gross.

NICK: Did you get upset?

GEROME reaches into both his pockets and pulls out two dripping fistfuls of roast beef.

MARION: Oh, look—leftover roast beast.

REID: Wimpy-ass veggie after all. Bedtime, Mikey. Say goodbye.

MICHAEL: Wait.

(to GEROME) Show them.

GEROME gives the meat to MARION. MARION awkwardly accepts it.

MARION: Ah—yep, sure.

GEROME takes some space. He tries a cartwheel and fails. He lies splayed out on his back where he landed. A pause.

GEROME: I want to stay the night.

Blackout.

SCENE TWO

Later that Friday night. GEROME is flossing in the bathroom. He wears sweatpants, his jacket, and his tie. MICHAEL is in pyjamas and drinking a can of cola.

MICHAEL: . . . My mom's like, "Keep it in the top of the toilet so Stinky doesn't find it." Marion's not actually stinky, but that's what my mom and I call her—

MICHAEL offers the can to GEROME.

Want some?

GEROME shakes his head and keeps on flossing.

What meds are you on? Do you have any Ritalin? I got some from the kid across the street—it's pretty much the best—then we got caffeine pills from his older sister and I was shaking for like two whole weeks, so now I only do this stuff—

MICHAEL gestures to the cola.

How many girlfriends have you had?

GEROME keeps flossing.

GEROME: Fi—wa—two—

MICHAEL: What—how many? Do you know what a newt is? It's like a water lizard—I'll trade you mine for your meds. Deal?

GEROME keeps flossing.

GEROME: Um.

MICHAEL: Deal. Do you have any tattoos? I have like three I want already but I'm not allowed till I'm sixteen. One of them I drew myself and it's sort of Hercules inspired, but like Hercules at the turn of the next millennium, and I showed Marion and she's like, "That's Justin Bieber with his shirt off." And I'm like, "No, it's not." She's like, "Yes, it is and it's really good." I'm like, "STINKY! SO STINKY!" Seriously, man, as soon as I have enough money, I'm outta here. I need my space. Do you have tattoos?

GEROME shakes his head.

Wait here.

MICHAEL exits. GEROME stops flossing. He regards himself in the mirror, then opens his mouth wide as if he's screaming and trying to look down his throat at the same time. He goes back to flossing. MICHAEL enters with a permanent marker.

You're a super dedicated flosser—I like that.

MICHAEL moves in front of GEROME with the marker. GEROME backs away.

One question: Do you wanna be a badass?

GEROME hesitates, then takes a big chug of MICHAEL's cola. He finishes the can and tosses it to the ground. He crouches to let MICHAEL write on his forehead.

Yeah! F-U-C—

MARION enters and grabs the marker.

MARION: MICHAEL!

MICHAEL: In case we lose him again, tell the cops we're looking for the guy with "Fu—"

MARION: "FUN!" The boy with "fun" written on him, and he's not the only one—

MARION uses the mirror and writes carefully on her forehead.

I'm right here beside you, Geromey—my forehead too.

MARION writes "FUN," but it's backwards. REID enters playing on an iPad.

REID: *(to MARION)* I thought I was checking on them.

MARION presents her forehead to REID.

MARION: Ta-daaaa!

REID: What'd you do to your face? "NUF"?

MARION: "FUN," Reid! We're having so much "FUN!"

MICHAEL grabs the marker and starts drawing on his forehead.

(to GEROME) Guess what would be even more fun? Why don't we give your mom a call and see if she's free for dinner tomorrow night! Would you like that?

MICHAEL: *(re: GEROME)* Wait—where's he sleeping?

REID: The bottom bunk—quit drawing shit on yourself.

MICHAEL: Which bottom bunk?

REID: Only one bottom bunk in the house.

MICHAEL: Why are you making me sleep with him?

MARION: Uncle Nick'll be there on the air mattress.

(to GEROME, too loudly) GIVE IT A THINK AND YOU LET ME KNOW, OKAY?

MICHAEL: What if he flips out?

MARION: We know it might be scary—

REID: He's not scared.

MICHAEL: Yes I am.

MARION: Go get your bike helmet. If it can protect you from cement, it can protect you from Geromey.

MICHAEL: Christ.

MARION: LANGUAGE, MICHAEL!

   MICHAEL points at the drawing on his forehead.

MICHAEL: It's "Hercules 3000" to you!

   REID shakes his head and chuckles at him.

(voice cracking) Fuck off, Dad.

   MICHAEL storms out.

MARION: *(calling after him)* Watch your mouth!

REID: *(calling after him)* Was that your voice cracking?

MARION: *(calling after him)* What kind of example are you for your cousin?

REID: *(calling after him)* Yeah, thirteen years old and your balls haven't dropped yet!

MARION comes at REID with the marker.

Get away from me!

MARION: *(to GEROME)* How'd your uncle look with an Aunt Marion original on his face?

REID sees GEROME nodding.

REID: Gimme that!

REID exits with the marker. GEROME starts brushing his teeth.

MICHAEL: *(off)* REEEEION! WHERE'S MY HELMET?

MARION: *(calling off)* WHERE YOU LEFT IT!

Pause.

MICHAEL: *(off)* MARIOOOON!

MARION: *(calling off)* MICHAEL!

MICHAEL: *(off)* I CAN'T FIND IT!

MARION: Oh golly.

MARION exits. GEROME stops brushing his teeth and starts floss-ing again. NICK can be heard on his cell as he approaches. He hangs back from the bathroom as he speaks.

NICK: *(off, to cell)* Come on, Toby, call in sick, come down and be here when he meets her . . . Fine, sulk by yourself at home . . . Toby, when we agreed to let Gerome decide, it meant he could say, "Yes! I do want to meet my birther!" That's his name for her, not mine . . . Look, I've seen massive changes in him already on this trip—he's in everyone's face, talkative—he loves it. The campsite is pretty niiii— Actually, we decided to spend the night at Reid and Marion's . . .

As NICK is on the phone, GEROME finds a pair of scissors. He looks at himself in the mirror and cuts off his tie right below the knot.

(off, to cell) Because, Toby, they're family and Gerome wants to stay with them . . . He's handling them very well . . . Yes, I'm also handling them very well.

NICK enters the bathroom.

(to cell) Sure, ask him yourself.

NICK takes in GEROME's cut tie.

(to GEROME, offering cell) Dad wants to do a check-in.

GEROME waves twice, "hello" and "goodbye."

What happened to your tie?

GEROME: It broke.

NICK: *(to cell)* Gerome says "hi-bye" . . . I dunno, the tie you gave him ripped.

MARION enters.

(to cell) I gotta go . . . Yep, bye.

(to GEROME) Dad says, "love." And he might come down.

MARION hands NICK a marker.

MARION: *(whispering)* Write something on your forehead so he doesn't feel left out.

NICK hands the marker back to MARION.

NICK: *(to GEROME)* Almost ready for bed?

MARION: You know what Geromey suggested?

MARION gives GEROME a wink.

And I'm thrilled! We're gonna invite his mama for dinner tomorrow!

NICK: *(to GEROME)* You want that?

GEROME stops flossing, nods, and immediately goes back to flossing.

MARION: Don't you think that's enough flossing?

NICK: Marion—

MARION: Sorry! Sorry!

GEROME: "Poor personal hygiene"—a telltale symptom of an in-patient.

NICK: You're not an in-patient.

MARION: But keep flossing—why not?

NICK holds out his cell.

NICK: If she's coming for dinner, you better call and introduce yourself.

GEROME shakes his head.

MARION: You want me to call?

NICK looks at her.

(to GEROME) You know what? You do it. Ooooh! We are gonna have such a special day tomorrow!

MARION goes to exit but stops, picking up the empty cola can.

Michael!

MARION yells off at MICHAEL as she leaves.

MICHAEL! SODA POP IS ROTTING YOUR BRAIN! SODA POP IS NOT THE ANSWER!

MARION exits, but then sticks her head back in.

Nighty-night!

And MARION is gone. GEROME stops flossing.

GEROME: Why doesn't Dad want me to meet my birther?

NICK: Dad wants you to know you can change your mind. The trip won't be a waste. You and I'll go camping and—

GEROME: I wish I came by myself.

NICK: You're not really talking to anyone, so it might be kinda tricky if you were here alone. And I wanna be here. If that makes any difference.

GEROME: I'm moving out next summer.

NICK: We said we'd talk about you moving out *sometime*.

GEROME: Seriously, man, I need my space—

NICK: *(imitating)* Yeah totally, man—

GEROME: Papa! If you're not gonna take me seriously, go home.

NICK: I love that you wanna be independent. But if I go back to Montreal, who's gonna make first contact?

> *NICK holds out the phone. GEROME won't take it.*

Are you scared of her or the phone? You can be scared of talking to her—I'm petrified. But the phone itself—not scary, perfectly safe. Don't play into the delusions.

GEROME: I can still hate cellular communication devices but recognize they won't suck out my thoughts and broadcast them to a quasi-merciful alien archangel named Serotonin.

NICK: Nope, no thought-sucking alien–angel things here—serotonin's a neuro brain chemical.

GEROME: *(correcting)* Neurotransmitter.

NICK: Yeah, exactly, let's focus on what's real—

GEROME: My hatred of cellphones! Pills, please.

NICK ignores the request.

NICK: Let's use this trip as a commitment to healthy living. You said you wanted to try to eat vegan, no sugar, no caffeine, we're gonna spend time in nature—

GEROME: What is with you and camping?

NICK: Like we used to.

GEROME: You've taken me camping twice. In my entire life.

GEROME holds out his hand.

Pills. Please.

After a moment of hesitation, NICK hands him a bottle of pills.

Dad takes them out for me.

GEROME fumbles to open the pill bottle.

NICK: Is this what you want your healed self to look like?

GEROME: What else is my healed self gonna look like?

GEROME opens the pill bottle and shakes one out into his palm.

They make me squeeze everything I am through a pinhole and it doesn't fit. But this weekend is too big, and Dad says, "Take your pills—"

NICK: "Your pills are what help." Uh-huh. And the doctors have given you this big diagnosis. Which just means they've caught up. Because you've been getting by your whole life without their help.

GEROME: Papa. If it was you and me in a tent until the year 2362 when they launch the *Enterprise*, I'd never have to worry. You could handle me and my voices. Did you see how they were looking at me at dinner?

NICK: No, no—

GEROME: Yes, they were! What's my birther gonna see?

NICK: I want her to see you.

GEROME: Imagine there's a pill given to me by an archalien—

NICK: I don't wanna talk about alien-angels with you. We're focusing on tactile, known things—

GEROME: Then imagine a black hole—it spits out a pill then it speaks to me—

NICK: Gerome—

GEROME: "This pill will make you like them for one day—one single day—before it tears your insides apart as it crushes you." I'd take the pill.

NICK: Be like us for more than a day. Be like us for the whole weekend! We have an opportunity—

GEROME: To meet the woman genetically responsible for me.

NICK: Yes, of course, but maybe—maybe—you're finding another way. There are survivors out there, no medication, walking around as if nothing ever happened.

GEROME closes the pill bottle and starts shaking it.

This could be relapse prevention—it could be relapse elimination—you and me and no antipsychotics.

GEROME stops shaking the pill bottle and shakes his head. He opens the bottle and takes a pill and puts it in his mouth. He stares at himself in the mirror.

Where are you?

GEROME: Right here. Talking to archangels and black holes.

GEROME spits the pill out and takes the cell from NICK. GEROME makes a swift, ritualized gesture that he has created to make the phone safe.

Number?

NICK hands GEROME a crumpled piece of paper. GEROME unfolds it and dials.

Captain's log, stardate 45944.1: a momentous occasion—

NICK: Is it ringing?

GEROME nods.

GEROME: A Starfleet officer making his first cellular voice communication in centuries to seek out new—

GEROME freezes.

NICK: ... Is it still ringing?

GEROME shakes his head vigorously. He opens his mouth, but nothing comes out. NICK mouths, "SAY HELLO." GEROME shakes his head and holds the phone out to NICK.

(to cell) Hello? Is this Saski? Oh—this is—my name's Nicholas Pinel—calling . . . I met you with my husband. About seventeen years ago. We adopted—ah . . . Yeah . . . Hi. We got your contact information from the agency. They said it would be okay if we contacted you and—um—we're actually in Thunder Bay. We were gonna camp and then—anyway, we're hoping, would you be willing toooo meet us? Gerome and I—my son and me? You don't have to answer. You can think about it . . .

NICK *nods, smiling at* GEROME.

Great, that's—you're gonna make him real happy . . . Ah. Actually. My brother and his wife want you to come over. For food. Tomorrow—probably seven-thirty—um, hold on a sec—

NICK *turns on the speakerphone. A young woman's voice—* SASKI—*fills the room.*

SASKI: *(from cell)* Nicholas? Are you there?

NICK: I put you on speaker.

SASKI: *(from cell)* Is he with you?

GEROME *shakes his head.*

NICK: He's already gone to bed.

SASKI: *(from cell)* You called me. Incredible. I had decided you never would. But I'm in the middle—

NICK: Is this a bad time?

SASKI: *(from cell)* I have to—yes—have to run. Tomorrow—

NICK: It's short notice—

SASKI: *(from cell)* Should be fine. What can I bring?

NICK: No—

SASKI: *(from cell)* Allergies or dietary restrictions?

NICK looks at GEROME. GEROME shakes his head.

NICK: Gerome's vegan.

SASKI: *(from cell)* Noted. Text your brother's address.

NICK: Okay, right—we'll see ya—

SASKI: *(from cell)* Nicholas? How is he? Is he well?

NICK: He's doing great.

SASKI: I'm looking forward to meeting him. Good night.

GEROME: *(to cell, quietly)* Bye.

NICK hangs up.

Thank you.

NICK: Uh-huh.

GEROME gives NICK the pill bottle.

GEROME: I'm not sure what I want my healed self to look like.

REID enters. His shirt is open and he's written "I'm with stupid" on his chest, with an arrow on his forehead pointing to one side.

REID: Where'd she go? Where's Marion?

NICK: Better cook us up another roast beast, Reidy boy. Company's coming.

REID: *(calling off)* HEY, MARION!

REID exits.

NICK puts the pill bottle on the counter and a hand on GEROME.

NICK: It's your choice, bud.

NICK hesitates for a moment, looking at the pill bottle. He exits.

GEROME picks up the pill bottle. He looks at himself in the mirror and pockets the pills.

MICHAEL enters covered from head to toe in sports pads and wearing a helmet.

MICHAEL: Precautionary measures, guy. I know you don't wanna flip out.

MICHAEL puts down a yogourt container and points at it.

His name's Alexander, but he won't respond when you call. He's actually the red-belly kind—pretty like sought after or whatever if you're into lizards of the water. Trial run. You wanna keep him, pill payment's due in twenty-four hours . . . I'll see you in there, I guess. Top bunk's mine.

MICHAEL kisses his fingers and gives GEROME two quick, gentle slaps on the cheek. GEROME stops brushing. MICHAEL exits. GEROME brushes. He stops and peeks under the lid of the container. Blackout.

SCENE THREE

Early Saturday morning. The sounds of mild, hetero porn. REID is at the dining table with his iPad. His shirt is open and he still has "I'm with stupid" on his chest. He's drinking beer and has a few empties beside him. GEROME enters. He is fully dressed in his suit jacket and tie, complete with meat-stained pants. He is finishing one of MICHAEL's cans of cola. He is noticeably more animated than the night before.

REID: Shit Michael looks up on this thing.

REID shoves the iPad in GEROME's face.

Did you know what those were at thirteen?

GEROME: I don't know what those are now.

REID: Fucking right, man—neither do I.

GEROME: What are you doing?

REID: It's four A.M.

GEROME waits.

So. Not sleeping. Obviously.

GEROME: Michael's snoring—my papa too—

REID: Runs in the family. You get off easy not being related—remember that.

GEROME: May I have a beer, please?

REID: Absolutely not. Have another pop. Or better yet, get yourself a glass of water.

GEROME exits. REID goes back to his iPad. The porn starts playing again, accidentally.

Fuck!

GEROME: *(off)* UNCLE, WE SHOULD MAKE THIS A "MAN'S HOUR."

REID: *(calling off)* WHAT THE HELL'S THAT?

GEROME enters with another cola.

GEROME: Time for us guys.

REID: *(re: can of cola)* That stuff's gonna keep you up.

GEROME: And rot my brain. Or it would for most people. I'm immune.

GEROME sits at the table and stares at REID.

REID: Can I help you?

GEROME: Man's hour. I'll go first. Once I went to my psychoanalyst, he gave me a picture of a painting—this man's head: totally hairless, pronounced bone. He'd most definitely undergone electric shock therapy six to eight billion times. The painting's a town too, growing over his skin like a rash—fields for cheeks, church out of an eye socket. A self-portrait by a patient—one look, I thought, "Nutter." Promised myself I'd be a more discrete nutjob.

REID: You're a chatty fucking Cathy before the sun comes up, huh?

GEROME: This is what man's hour is all about. The next week the nutjob's self-portrait's in my forehead: popped up overnight like a whitehead. He wanted me to kill him—he said so himself. I wanted to kill him, so at least there was consensus. I went at him with a pair of toenail clippers. Snip, snip, snip. Gush. Oops. "There goes the neighbourhood, dear." "That poor boy the gays are raising—he's lost himself completely." Mantra number twenty-three: throw out your toenail clippers. Mantra number seven: don't see their faces, don't hear their voices. Make the choice not to. Uncle Reid?

REID: No, "screw it"—that's the new mantra. Don't worry about the voices. And forget the shrink who told you to worry about the voices. Another place, another time—you'd be the damn shaman of this village—those voices would be our ancestor spirits or some spectral-ass shit.

REID goes back to his iPad.

Shaman it, my man. Fuck, I hate solitaire.

REID gets up and grabs his jacket.

GEROME: *(speaking Klingon) Heghlu'meH QaQ jajvam—*

REID: What'd you say?

GEROME: "Man's hour: freedom, the spirit soars."

REID: Was that . . . Klingon?

GEROME: I think I might be sugar drunk.

REID: Go back to bed. You'll be fine in the morning.

GEROME: Where are you going?

REID: Booze run.

GEROME: I'll drive.

REID: Do you know how?

GEROME: You can teach me.

REID: That's your papa's job.

GEROME: Are you a better driver?

REID: Of course.

GEROME: I want you to teach me.

REID: Not at four A.M.!

GEROME: More man time!

REID: Go to bed. It's me time now.

GEROME: You weren't watching pornography when I came in, were you?

REID: Oh, you little fucker—it's called porn! Thanks for interrupting.

GEROME: I'm eighteen. Driving's a useful skill.

REID: You're seventeen—

GEROME: Almost eighteen.

REID: Learning how to sleep through the night's a fucking useful skill too.

GEROME: Shaman wants to learn to drive, Uncle. Don't hold me back.

REID groans.

REID: Find your papa's key. Fucked if I'm teaching you on my car.

A shift. NICK's car. GEROME is in the driver's seat while REID sits shotgun. GEROME looks at him.

Well ... Turn it on.

GEROME: How?

REID: Don't be a 'tard. Turn on the goddamn car.

GEROME starts the car.

GEROME: I want to be cautious: most teenagers are accused of being rash.

REID: Don't let them call you names, shaman. You can go faster.

GEROME: We're not moving yet.

REID: Yeah. Go. Faster.

GEROME: What's the speed limit?

REID: It's my fucking driveway—the speed limit's whatever the hell I want it to be—

GEROME: Where are we going?

REID: Twenty-four-hour beer vending machine at the Old Country Motel. Straight, and I'll tell you when to turn. Move it, Gerome—speed up!

GEROME: This is basically fifty—

REID: It's forty-five. The speed limit's sixty, no one goes under seventy, AND the only good part about driving at four A.M. is the road's yours, so own it.

GEROME: Okay, what else? Teach me more.

REID: What the fuck? Whataya want from me? Drive.

GEROME: This is it?

REID: You're driving. You're doing it. Keep doing it.

GEROME: How do I turn?

REID: You turn—

GEROME *begins to turn and* REID *grabs the wheel.*

NOT NOW! At a cross street, asswipe.

GEROME: How do I brake?

REID: You—

GEROME *slams on the brakes and they both jolt forwards.*

Yep, you got it. Turn right up here.

GEROME: This is super—you are such a good teacher.

REID: Best uncle ever, riding shotgun—turn, the motel. Turn! What the fuck? You missed it!

GEROME: Look how fast I'm going now! Pretty good, huh?

REID: Do a uey and take me back to my beer machine.

GEROME rolls down the window and lets out a howl.

Okay, stop the car—

GEROME speeds up so fast REID is thrown back.

That's not the brake!

GEROME: Do you know any Klingon? "*Jajvam*" roughly translated is "today"—

REID: You need to slow down!

GEROME: "*MeH QaQ*," that's "is a good day"—

REID: Are you losing it on me right now?

GEROME: Want to see my impression of myself obliterating?

REID: No— What?

GEROME takes his hands from the steering wheel, covers his eye, and screams.

REID grabs the wheel.

Don't ever, ever take your hands off the wheel!

GEROME takes the wheel back.

GEROME: That's the first thing you actually taught me!

REID: Why are you looking at me? Look at the road!

GEROME: You know what my favourite *Star Trek* moment ever is?

REID sees something ahead and grabs for the wheel.

REID: NO, WATCH OUT!

GEROME sees it too.

GEROME: Oh shit.

A blinding flash—and then blackout.

SCENE FOUR

The sound of porn picks up where it left off as the lights shift. It's later Saturday morning. MICHAEL is eating a bowl of cereal and watching the iPad. MARION enters.

MARION grabs the iPad and struggles to stop the video.

MARION: MICHAEL! What did we say about watching your father's movies? This is coming right out of your screen time allowance, young man.

MICHAEL: My body's going through changes, Reeon—I have questions.

NICK enters from upstairs.

MARION: Turn off the smut and ask me, I'm happy to answer anything.

MICHAEL moves closer to the iPad.

MICHAEL: Okay—

MICHAEL grabs the iPad, presses play again, and shoves it in MARION's face.

Can I have $12.99 for a subscription?

MARION covers her eyes.

MARION: Don't!

MICHAEL keeps going.

MICHAEL: New videos in your inbox every day of the week!

MICHAEL exits with the porn playing as he goes. MARION sees NICK.

MARION: I'm not his mother—what am I supposed to do?

NICK: Um . . . Can I make coffee?

MARION grabs an envelope.

MARION: You sit. Before you open it—normally there'd be more—how much has Reid told you?

NICK: Nothing—we don't talk.

MARION: We gave them another fifteen thousand—oh my god, that's a queasy feeling, isn't it? That's forty-five thousand in all—on me, on this—

MARION puts a hand on her belly.

This time around they've given us a twenty-five percent chance of fertilization, and they've assured us that they're being conservative with that estimate—

MARION holds out the envelope.

All that's my excuse for this being so light. But I bet it's still better than a bar cowboy.

NICK doesn't take it.

This is how we help you. Let us help you.

NICK: I didn't even know you were trying.

MARION puts the envelope on the table.

MARION: Oh, stop, don't worry about me.

MARION sits. A slight pause.

I don't know what I'll do if it doesn't work this time.

NICK: Adoption?

MARION: Oh, I think it's so great that you and Toby did. Why not, right? But for me, you know, ah . . . Yeah, you understand.

MARION stands again.

Coffeeeee! And oh! Oh! I forgot to tell you, Nicky. You have to stay till Monday.

MARION exits to the kitchen.

NICK: *(calling off)* WHY?

MARION: *(off)* IT'S MICHAEL'S SCHOOL PLAY!

NICK: *(calling off)* OH—SURE.

MARION: *(off)* REALLY?

NICK: *(calling off)* NO.

MARION enters with two coffees and hands one to NICK.

MARION: They're doing a theatrical version of *Paradise Lost* by Sir Johnny Milton and Ms. Blueberry, a remarkable grade eight teacher—her class is so advanced. I'm the props mistress—golden snakes and apples, evergreen halos—that's the kind of look we're going for. And and and! The kids are all making their own costumes! I want it to be a complete surprise. I'm not letting Michael show me his before the big day.

NICK: Who's he playing?

MARION: Paradise—title role.

NICK: I didn't realize Paradise was an actual character.

MARION: He and Lost are the narrators.

(calling off) MICHAEL! BRING YOUR SCRIPT! WE'LL DO A LITTLE SHOW FOR YOUR UNCLE!

> *REID enters from upstairs. His nose is bloody and covered with a crudely applied bandage.*

REID: Where's coffee?

> *MARION lets out three short, piercing screams, one after the other.*

(overlapping screams) I'm fine, I'm fine—shut up!

(re: nose) It's nothing.

> *MICHAEL enters, running, with his headphones on.*

NICK: What happened?

> *GEROME enters from upstairs. He's still wearing his suit jacket, tie, and stained pants.*

REID: *(re: GEROME)* This is all his fault.

GEROME: I can make it better.

NICK: *(to REID)* What did you do?

REID: No, it's what your fucking dashboard did to my nose.

NICK: Oh god.

REID takes MARION's coffee.

MARION: *(to REID)* Please tell me you went to the hospital.

REID slaps GEROME on the back.

REID: Who needs a fucking hospital? But Gerome here is a shitty-ass driver—

NICK: You drove?

MICHAEL: *(to GEROME)* You crashed? Awesome!

MARION: No! Not awesome!

(to REID) You let him drive? Are you insane?

MICHAEL: LANGUAGE!

NICK: He doesn't have a licence.

GEROME: I told him I did.

NICK: *(to REID)* You're the adult! You should know better!

NICK looks out the window.

Where the hell is it?

REID: We sacrificed the car to save Bambi, who didn't look both ways before crossing.

NICK: Fuck.

REID: Sadly, Bambi didn't make it either.

NICK: The car's not even mine—it's Toby's!

REID: It's perfectly salvageable—we just need to pound down the hood and replace the front bumper—it's waiting for you in a ditch six blocks down.

    NICK grabs his jacket.

NICK: Why didn't you call a tow truck?

REID: We don't need one—I got chains for the pickup, we'll do it ourselves. Look, man, it was pitch black—

(re: GEROME) And this one was looking a little frayed around the edges—I figured I'd make the ADULT decision and get him home.

GEROME: Papa—

NICK: Not now—your uncle and I are going to find your dad's car.

GEROME: Papa, please let me fix this.

NICK: No, you're staying.

GEROME: But what about the deer?

NICK: What about the deer?

GEROME: What's happening to him?

NICK: I thought you said you killed it.

GEROME: Yeah.

NICK: So that's what's happening to it.

> *NICK pockets the envelope of money. NICK and REID exit from the house.*

> *MARION and GEROME stare at each other.*

> *GEROME turns and starts to exit upstairs.*

> *MICHAEL pulls off his headphones.*

MICHAEL: Hercules! Help me memorize!

> *GEROME looks to MARION, who hesitates for just a moment.*

MARION: Okay! Where are the pants I gave you? You gotta dress different to feel different, Gerome. I'm getting you new sweats and some cereal!

> *MARION exits.*

MICHAEL: Duder—quick—what's your mom's name?

GEROME: Saski Halton . . . Mom.

> *MICHAEL starts typing into the iPad.*

MICHAEL: "S-A—"

GEROME: "S-K-I."

MICHAEL: Skiiiiiii. You sad about the deer?

GEROME only shrugs—but he is. He downs the rest of NICK's coffee.

Whoa, dude! You're super dedicated to coffee, I—

GEROME: Does Alexander the newt eat?

MICHAEL: He eats like the finest quality pellets money can buy from Noah's Pet and Supply Shop—you want some? Cuz that's gonna cost even more pills, and you haven't paid me for the newt. I don't want you getting high off my asking price.

GEROME: They're safe. I'm on an antipsychotic break—a cleanse.

MICHAEL offers GEROME the iPad.

MICHAEL: Wanna see your mom's picture?

GEROME: Seen it.

GEROME takes the iPad and starts searching for something.

MICHAEL: I could show you the costume I'm making!

GEROME shrugs and starts to down MARION's coffee.

Hey, give me some of that!

GEROME gives him the coffee. MICHAEL tries a sip but he clearly doesn't like it and hands it back.

You wanna scare Marion with me?

GEROME doesn't respond.

Yeah you do! Act like you're flipping out! Do some crazy shit!

GEROME plays a song on the iPad—"Mama Said" by the Shirelles. GEROME starts singing along. He knows it by heart.

What the hell's this?

MICHAEL listens to the song and then starts laughing.

Aw! Mama's coming! Mama Gerome! Come on, come on, come on, Mama!

MICHAEL starts dancing. He pulls GEROME up. MICHAEL dances around GEROME as GEROME barely sways. MICHAEL kisses GEROME on the cheek. MICHAEL goes back to dancing. MICHAEL goes in for another kiss, but pulls back as MARION enters, running. She has clean clothes, a bowl of cereal, and a laundry basket full of Styrofoam balls, some of which have been painted gold.

MARION: STOP STOP STOP! NO DANCING WITHOUT ME!

MARION joins in—she dances exuberantly and sings along loudly. MICHAEL makes sure to dance apart from her. MARION sits, exhausted, and picks up the iPad.

Oooh! Sssassskeeeaaahhhh. Lakehead University—Ph.D.!

GEROME tries to take the iPad from her, but MARION holds it away from him, reading.

Gawd, she looks like she's twelve. "An associate professor in the Department of Anthropology, Dr. Halton"—oh, boy! We better buy some coffee-table books so it looks like we read things. Cereal—check! Clean clothes—check! Golden apples—check! Oh oh oh, Geromey! How about you make your papa a "sorry I crashed the car" apple!

MICHAEL stops dancing and picks up a ball.

MICHAEL: You'd have to be high to believe these are gold.

MARION: If they believe you're Paradise, they'll believe my apples.

MICHAEL dumps the basket of golden apples and they scatter everywhere.

MICHAEL!

MICHAEL: Paradise rampage with crappy foam!

MICHAEL starts tossing the golden apples at GEROME as MARION tries to pick them up.

Gold bounces right off you—Heeeeercules!

GEROME starts to throw them back.

MARION: Boys!

MICHAEL: Heeeeercules with crappy aim! Right here! No, here! Maybe I'm only in your head!

MARION grabs MICHAEL's wrist and forces him to sit in a chair.

MARION: You. Stop.

MICHAEL: What's your problem?

MARION: Gerome, go change.

GEROME starts changing in the middle of the room. He takes off his shirt, and his chest and arms are completely covered with words written in permanent marker.

MARION shakes her head.

Oh—wash that off.

GEROME: These are my mantras.

MARION: I don't care.

MICHAEL holds one of GEROME's arms and reads.

MICHAEL: "Have sexual intercourse"?

GEROME: I may be the only seventeen-year-old in existence who has not had sex.

GEROME grabs the bowl of cereal and starts eating it loudly. Throughout the following there is an element of performance to what GEROME is doing, and MARION is unsure if she should take it seriously.

MARION: Gerome. You're so, so ... young.

GEROME: *(in Klingon)* Heghlu'meH—

MARION: *QaQ jajvam.* Don't pull that Klingon junk with me. I was singing the songs of Kronos before you were born.

MICHAEL: *(to GEROME)* Teach me Klingon!

GEROME: *(to MARION)* How much do you like *Star Trek*?

MARION: I'm not a Trekkie anymore.

GEROME: My dad Toby likes it the most—I'm worried I don't like it as much as I used to.

MARION: Sounds like you know pretty much all there is to know about it, so—

GEROME: That doesn't mean I like it—

GEROME gestures to the mantras.

Now you know pretty much all there is to know about me doesn't mean you like me. It's one more check on the list of possible symptoms: "you will stop finding pleasure in what was once pleasurable." Maybe I won't even like sex when I have it.

MARION: I really don't know, but I am asking you for the last time—

GEROME puts his shirt back on.

GEROME: Sorry sorry sorry sorry sorry sorry—

MARION: Go clean yourself!

GEROME: Brain cleaning, yes! Clean the neurotransmitters with tires and make them roadkill—

For a moment, GEROME is distracted, moving his lips silently.

MARION: Gerome. Stop. Gerome? Can you hear me?

GEROME: Yes.

MARION: Are you hearing anything else right now? Any voices?

GEROME: I'm always hearing voices.

MARION: Can you talk to them? Reason with them?

GEROME: Ha!

MARION grabs his shoulders.

MARION: Excuse me in there! Hello? Gerome is a nice boy and I want you all to stop bothering him! Leave my nephew alone!

MICHAEL: Jesus, Reedong.

MARION: What do those voices of yours say to that?

GEROME: They say I'm going to die.

MARION: But you look so healthy. They're the crazy ones, not you.

GEROME: They say you are going to kill me.

MARION: I'm going to what?

MICHAEL: Ummmm, that's freaky. And pretty cool.

Again, for a moment, GEROME's lips move silently.

MARION: *(to MICHAEL, snapping her fingers)* Come over here.

MICHAEL: No.

MARION: Give your cousin some space.

(to GEROME) I'm not going to hurt you.

GEROME: You'll do it with your eyes.

MARION: I'm not magic—I'm not a witch.

GEROME: Who said anything about magic. You'll use your eyes to kill me: no magic—eyes. I have to defend myself to the death.

MARION grabs her phone.

MARION: . . . Is what the voices say.

GEROME: Oh, these voices won't hurt us.

GEROME moves his lips silently again. MARION dials 911.

This is kid's stuff, a little background din. I've been vanquishing voices like this since kindergarten.

MARION: Uh-huh, keep telling me . . .

(to cell) Ambulance, I need an ambulance—

GEROME: *(shouting into cell)* No no no no no!

GEROME continues to shout "NO" over MARION.

MARION: Just keep talking to me, Gerome!

(to cell) Marion Pinel, 305 Southgate Court . . .

GEROME: *(shouting overtop)* Don't send an ambulance!

MARION: . . . He's got schizophrenia . . .

MICHAEL: *(shouting overtop)* She's the crazy one! She's mental!

MARION: *(to cell)* . . . He's having a breakdown. He's my nephew—

REID and NICK enter from outside. NICK is on his cell.

REID: *(to MARION)* We got a tow truck to take it to the shop. Fucking rip-off—

NICK: *(to cell)* . . . I don't know how it happened, Toby. I didn't see the deer—

GEROME: PAPA!

NICK: *(covering phone, to GEROME)* Not now—

MICHAEL: *(to REID)* DAD! Your wife called 911!

NICK: *(to cell)* Call you back. Yep—bye.

(to MARION) You did WHAT?

> MARION *tosses* NICK *a blanket.*

MARION: Wrap Gerome up!

GEROME: She thinks I'm flipping out—no no NO!

MARION: *(to NICK)* This is it! Look how worked up he is!

NICK: He's a teenager! That's what they do, get worked up! Most people tell them to go play outside before calling emergency.

REID: You boys need to blow off some steam?

NICK: Let's go run around the block.

REID: No, family fun time: we'll go hunting.

MARION: He stole his dad's car, crashed it, and you want to take him to the woods! He should be grounded!

NICK: I don't ground my son.

MARION: *(to cell)* Yes, I'm still here! Why aren't you sending someone?

(to NICK) He heard voices! Saying that I was going to kill him!

NICK: *(to GEROME)* Were the voices real?

GEROME shakes his head no.

GEROME: I knew right from the start.

MICHAEL: We're just making apples.

MICHAEL sits down and starts to work on an apple. GEROME follows his lead and begins working on an apple of his own. MICHAEL throws an apple at MARION and it bounces off her head.

MARION: *(to cell)* YES, I'M HERE! I don't know . . . No, don't send anyone. We're fine.

MARION hangs up and wraps herself in the blanket.

NICK's cell beeps—a text.

NICK checks his phone.

NICK: Saski. She's "looking forward to dinner tonight."

MICHAEL: Mama's coming!

Blackout.

SCENE FIVE

The woods, Saturday afternoon. REID *enters with his nose still bandaged holding a walkie-talkie. He appears to be tracking something.* NICK *follows carelessly with a sophisticated looking bow and arrow.*

NICK: . . . He can be a regular teenager. He goes between burying himself in my arms when his mind's playing tricks on him to insisting I walk ten paces behind him in public and only speak when spoken to. He'd be happy for the delusion that Toby and I do not exist—he lives on his own in an apartment, can metro downtown to gawk at the strip clubs on Saint Catherine, then go for poutine at two in the morning.

REID: Sounds like a delusion you should encourage.

REID stops suddenly, crouches, hits NICK, *and points off.*

NICK: Ow!

REID: Aim.

NICK: What?

REID: Aim, fuck.

NICK: Where?

REID straightens up—the target he's spotted has gone.

REID: Dammit! Why you gotta ruin my man's hour?

NICK: Your what hour?

REID: Look. Either Gerome's chowing cheese curds on his own, or you're his nurse for the rest of your life—choose your delusion.

NICK: No delusions—that's where we have to get to. Toby's started going to these support sessions for parents and they've got their buzzwords—treatment compliance, medication adherence—but what they know could fit on a single sheet of loose-leaf. It's like Toby's forgotten that we have been doing fine with Gerome for-for-for seventeen years without doctors, without anyone but the three of us. They'd never even heard of this herbal stuff—xingshen—that's supposed to help soothe him, and it's completely non-invasive—

REID: Hold on. What the shit? Are you planning on spending the money I give you on fucking Herbal Essences? Shampoo they're hocking at you like medicine?

NICK: I didn't know your money came with restrictions.

REID: It comes with an implicit "don't be a moron" clause.

NICK: You've seen him. The meds make him docile, sedentary, so he drinks coffee and pop and energy drinks all day just to feel normal, but then he's jittery, and with the jitters the hallucinations come back. So let's give him more pills to calm him down, maybe, until—

REID: All I'm saying is you gotta—

NICK: I can't lose him, Reid.

REID: Nick!

NICK: The doctors don't know how these pills work. The meds, the diagnosis, it all comes with an implicit "this could kill you" clause. Tons of people like Gerome die young.

REID: Okay, okay—

NICK: If I am going to outlive my son, then I will make these the best years I can.

REID: Nick—

NICK: But I . . . I don't know if I'm doing the right thing.

REID doesn't know what to say. Pause. MARION is heard shouting from off.

MARION: *(off)* CEASE FIRE! CEASE FIRE!

There's a sudden blast from an air horn.

REID: Are you shitting me?

MARION enters shouting, wearing bright clothing and a reflective safety vest, holding a walkie-talkie and brandishing an air horn.

MARION: CEASE YOUR FIRE! HUMANS IN THE BUSH!

REID: The fuck's wrong with you?

MARION: I didn't know it was you.

REID: What the hell are you doing in front of us? You're supposed to stay to our backs.

MARION: I'm looking for the boys.

REID: That's what the fucking walkie-talkie is for, beautiful.

MARION: No response!

REID: *(into the walkie-talkie)* MIKEY!

MICHAEL and GEROME enter. GEROME has a backpack. MICHAEL has the extendable baton and is imagining it is a machete.

MICHAEL: . . . Okay, if you're the admiral of Starfleet, I'm Captain—

MICHAEL sees the others.

What?

REID: *(to MARION)* Magic! They come when I call.

MARION: I lost you two.

MICHAEL: We're using the buddy system. Gerome and I are safer without you.

REID: *(to MICHAEL, re: shooting)* You wanna give it a try?

MICHAEL grabs GEROME by the hand and starts leading him off.

MICHAEL: Naw, Dad, we're going to the lake!

REID: The lake! We're on a goddamn hunting expedition!

MICHAEL and GEROME exit.

MARION: *(calling after)* Wait!

NICK: *(calling after)* Ten more minutes—that's it! We gotta make dinner.

MARION: *(calling after)* For Mommy!

NICK moves to follow after them.

NICK: I don't think they heard—

NICK gives the bow and arrow to REID.

REID: You're doing a good job, man. You are.

NICK nods and exits after them.

MARION: Are you giving your brother parenting advice?

REID has struck a pose with the bow and arrow. MARION laughs and shakes her head, then goes to follow NICK.

Where's the lake?

REID: How the fuck should I know?

MARION readies her air horn and starts calling all their names. REID and MARION exit together. After a moment, GEROME and MICHAEL enter. They are in another area of the woods.

GEROME: . . . We can only trust other members of Starfleet.

MICHAEL: Then Stinky's out. Stop—this is it. Doesn't really count as a lake, huh?

GEROME: It's water.

MICHAEL: It's a swamp.

GEROME: I really like it.

MICHAEL: Yeah, totally! The friggin' sweet spot—this is the only reason I come.

The air horn blasts again—they both look in the direction of the noise. It continues intermittently through the end of the scene.

GEROME: Can you hear a voice?

MICHAEL: Seriously? Like right now?

GEROME nods. GEROME takes the yogourt container out of his backpack.

GEROME: It's Alexander.

(playfully) "Let me go, Michael, let me go!"

MICHAEL: Oh, shut up. I don't care, he's your newt.

GEROME opens the container as if letting the newt go. Then he hands his pill bottle to MICHAEL. NICK and MARION can be heard calling their names.

GEROME: Bonus payment.

MICHAEL: All of them?

GEROME: All of them.

MICHAEL puts them in his pocket and leans his head on GEROME. The sound of the air horn and the voices calling continue into black.

SCENE SIX

Saturday night. MICHAEL is in the living room/dining room with the iPad and has his headphones on. He's dressed up. GEROME is there, talking to himself and extending his hand as if rehearsing an introduction.

MARION: *(off)* DID SOMEONE HEAR THE DOOR?

NICK: *(off)* SHE'S NOT SUPPOSED TO BE HERE FOR ANOTHER HOUR!

MARION: *(off)* REID! DID YOU SET THE TABLE?

REID: *(off)* MIKE! SET THE TABLE!

MICHAEL: GEROME! SET THE TABLE!

NICK enters, struggling with his tie.

NICK: *(to GEROME)* Everything under control? How we feeling?

GEROME nods. During the following, GEROME takes NICK's tie and ties it on himself expertly.

MARION: *(off)* NICK, HUN! IT'S FINE, BUT IS YOUR CASSEROLE SUPPOSED TO LOOK LIKE THIS?

NICK: *(calling off)* LIKE WHAT?

MARION: *(off)* LIKE THIS! I'M SURE IT'LL TASTE GREAT NO MATTER WHAT BUT COME LOOK!

NICK: Are we doing the right thing, Gerome?

GEROME kisses him on the cheek and puts the tie around his papa's neck. NICK exits to the kitchen.

MARION: *(off)* WAIT! I HEAR A CAR! THAT IS DEFINITELY A CAR!

MARION enters from the kitchen running. She's dressed up too.

MARION looks out the front window.

Oh my Jay—SHE'S EARLY!

(calling off) REID! MICHAEL!

MICHAEL: RYE-ON! I'M RIGHT HERE!

MARION: COMPUTER! OFF! POSITIONS, EVERYONE!

GEROME: *(to himself, quickly)* Hello my name's Gerome nice to meet—

MARION: First impressions, Gerome—please! Don't act . . . you know.

NICK enters from the kitchen, his cell ringing.

The food! We're not ready!

NICK: Let her wait.

(to cell) Toby?

MARION: *(calling off)* REID! WE NEED THAT OVEN ON FULL POWER, STAT!

MARION exits to the kitchen, running.

NICK: *(to cell)* Yeah, all good, Toby—little busy—but he's right here—

GEROME: I forgot to shower!

NICK: Too late now. You smell fine.

NICK offers the phone to GEROME.

Talk to your dad—

GEROME takes the cell as though it is contaminated and speaks to NICK.

GEROME: If I forget to wash myself, I'll forget to brush myself—

NICK: Okay, breathe—

GEROME: If I forget to brush myself, then I'll forget to wipe myself. If I forget to wipe myself, then on top of everything else, you'll have to clean up my shit!

NICK: *(quietly)* Tell your dad we'll call him—

GEROME does his gesture to make cellphones safe. He shouts into the cell, not bringing it close to his head.

GEROME: CALL YOU BACK, BYE!

GEROME hangs up.

NICK: This is what I'm talking about—are you in control?

GEROME: Yes! I don't want my mother smelling my shit!

GEROME exits upstairs, oblivious of the cell still in his hand.

NICK: Gerome! . . . Wash fast!

The doorbell rings, and rings again almost immediately. NICK looks at the door but he doesn't move. There's a knock.

(to MICHAEL) You get it.

NICK exits to the kitchen. MICHAEL opens the door and SASKI enters. She's in jeans and carries a platter and a plastic bag.

SASKI: Hello there, I'm—

MICHAEL: If I tell Gerome you're a *Star Trek* super fan and honorary Starfleet officer, he'll like you more.

SASKI: Ah-ha.

MICHAEL: It'll cost you, though.

GEROME enters from upstairs. His suit is soaking wet. He jumped in the shower fully dressed. MICHAEL sees him coming and hugs SASKI.

On behalf of Starfleet, welcome to our home, Professor.

GEROME pulls MICHAEL away from SASKI.

Ow!

SASKI and GEROME see each other for only a brief moment before REID enters, bringing NICK with him. REID's nose is still bandaged.

REID: Let's do the big howdy!

REID sees GEROME.

My suit! What the hell?

MICHAEL: Dad! Gerome pushed me!

NICK: *(to GEROME)* Apologize.

REID: Sorry, my son's a pussy.

NICK: Not you, him.

GEROME: *(to SASKI)* Sorry.

NICK: To Michael.

SASKI waves hello.

SASKI: Um . . .

REID: *(to SASKI)* So you're her, huh?

SASKI: Ah—yes?

GEROME: *(loudly, nervously)* MY NAME'S—

MARION enters from the kitchen, interrupting GEROME.

MARION: Hi! Welcome! Oh my goodness!

SASKI: I couldn't remember if we said six-thirty or seven—

NICK: We said seven-thirty—

MARION hugs SASKI.

MARION: It doesn't even matter. We're thrilled to have you. I'm blasting the tater tots, and we threw the casserole in the fire—ha-ha!

SASKI: It smells delicious. Who's the cook?

MARION: Nick, and I'm his number one.

SASKI: Let the kitchen know—typical me—I've double-booked myself tonight.

NICK: Seriously?

MARION: We were so last minute with the invitation.

SASKI: I'll leave before eight.

MARION: Of course—

SASKI: Fine if dinner's still going on. I'll sneak out. No one will notice.

(re: GEROME) Now is this . . .

MARION: Right! We didn't even work out how we were going to do this— Presenting—ta-da!

SASKI gives the platter and bag to NICK and takes GEROME's hand in both of hers.

SASKI: Really incredible to meet you.

(re: GEROME's suit) But I'm underdressed and too dry.

MARION: It's all Gerome—he's the fancy one!

SASKI offers the plastic bag to GEROME.

SASKI: Excuse the lazy wrapping.

GEROME pulls out an extra-large T-shirt that says Lakehead University.

I work there.

MICHAEL: We know. We stalked you online.

GEROME puts it on over his jacket—it's like a dress.

MARION: Aw, isn't that the most adorable—

GEROME pulls a wine bottle from the plastic bag.

SASKI: That's not for you—

NICK: I should've said about this place and wine—

MARION grabs the wine bottle.

MARION: This looks so good! Thank you!

SASKI: What about wine?

MARION: I don't know what about wine—wine what?

NICK: ... That you didn't have to bother because we've already got a bottle.

MARION: Well, that one's open and this one looks like it's gonna be—a spectacular experience.

MICHAEL takes the platter from NICK and tries to help himself.

MICHAEL: Can I have a doughnut?

MARION grabs the platter.

MARION: Michael, these are a Thunder Dome delicacy! I can't believe you brought Persians!

SASKI: They're homemade.

MARION: SHUT UP! Pink icing and everything!

SASKI: *(to GEROME)* Animal free, every crumb. I'm told you're vegan.

There's suddenly a piercing beep—the fire alarm.

NICK: What the hell is that?

MARION: THE FOOD! DAMN IT!

REID exits to the kitchen, running. MARION tries to run after him but bumps into NICK. The platter of Persians falls to the ground.

Oh my god!

MICHAEL: REEEEION!

MARION: Nick! Get out of the way!

MARION exits.

SASKI: *(calling off)* Do you need help?

NICK: *(calling off)* Do we need to run from the house screaming?

The fire alarm stops. MICHAEL kicks the Persians. GEROME pushes him away.

MICHAEL: Ow! Uncle N!

GEROME: Pick them up! We can still save them!

GEROME piles the pastries back onto the platter. SASKI begins to help. REID enters from the kitchen.

NICK: Leave it—

REID: Don't leave it, let him clean it up—

SASKI: Is everything all right in there?

MARION enters from the kitchen.

MARION: I am so sorry! I never drop things!

MARION helps clean the floor.

Oooh! Does *vaygen* stain?

SASKI: How's dinner?

MARION: The casserole's in critical condition.

REID nods towards the platter, clicking his tongue.

REID: Mikey, kitchen—

MICHAEL groans, takes the platter from GEROME, and exits to the kitchen.

MARION: Maybe let's brush those off!

MARION exits to the kitchen after him.

REID: Okay! So, welcome. We hope you survive.

REID exits to the kitchen.

SASKI: . . . That was your brother? And his wife?

NICK: Yeah, Reid, Marion, Michael's my nephew, and this is Gerome—obviously. You met already.

SASKI: Yes, of course—

SASKI laughs.

Hello. Again.

A slight pause.

I'm glad you like the shirt.

A slight pause.

Is there a washroom?

SASKI wiggles her fingers.

Icing.

NICK: Upstairs, end of the hall.

She exits upstairs.

GEROME: What did I do wrong?

NICK: You didn't do anything wrong.

GEROME: Everyone left.

NICK: They didn't leave cuz of you.

GEROME: "Watch out for personal hygiene." I showered. I did—

NICK: I know, bud.

GEROME: Do you think she likes me?

NICK: She met you two seconds ago.

GEROME: So?

NICK: So—I bet she liked you as soon as she saw you.

GEROME: I want to shower again.

> *GEROME starts moving his fingers in quick repetitive motions. It begins in one hand then spreads to both.*

NICK: Gerome? What if you want her to go?

GEROME: I'm not gonna want that.

NICK: What if you need her to go?

GEROME: Make them all come back—

NICK: Stop moving your fingers—

GEROME: It's keeping me focused on not listening.

NICK: To me? Or the voices?

GEROME: Both.

NICK: Is that getting harder?

GEROME: Everyone hears voices! I'm treated like I'm broken for admitting it!

NICK: We can reconsider. If we need to. Your pills.

GEROME: We made an agreement. You'd give me up so easily!

SASKI enters from upstairs.

I take those pills, you might as well tie me to a chair, lock me up—is that what you want?

NICK: No.

SASKI: Everything all right?

NICK: We're fine.

GEROME: *(to SASKI)* Do you have schizophrenia?

SASKI: No.

GEROME: You don't?

SASKI shakes her head.

I do.

SASKI: You—?

NICK: I was planning to work up to that.

SASKI: *(to GEROME)* I—I am sorry.

GEROME: Is it your fault?

SASKI: I didn't know.

NICK: I could've warned you.

SASKI: *(to GEROME)* You have ...

GEROME: Schizophrenia.

NICK: Doesn't change anything.

SASKI: Of course not. No ... You live with your fathers?

(to NICK) Big job.

NICK: He's essentially independent. I dunno how much you know about it—

SASKI: I'm no expert—

NICK: They think it's a disorder of the mind—

SASKI: I'm also not completely mental-health illiterate.

GEROME: Then what's "praecox"?

SASKI shakes her head.

(quickly) "*Dementia praecox*," Latin—the original term: intellectual degradation. Sounds so graceful: it isn't—

(re: NICK and SASKI) You have brains that are gracefully degrading. Anyone old has a brain that's proudly breaking down very, very, very slowly—mine's ripping at warp speed. It hasn't stopped expanding either: brains don't stop growing until you're twentysomething, meaning this isn't my full crazy. It has a couple of crushing years to

tear bigger, stronger, grow hair on its parts: imagine after my crazy goes through puberty.

SASKI: That is an incredible train of thought.

GEROME: They've never seen anything like me before: I'm different from all other people souls, plant souls, animal souls, universal atoms.

SASKI: The rest—all us same souls and atoms—must be pretty bland from your perspective.

GEROME: Did the human you had sex with to create me have it?

NICK: She doesn't—

(to SASKI) You don't have to talk about that—

    SASKI shakes her head.

SASKI: I believe that you're the first I've ever met.

GEROME: *(to SASKI)* Statistically speaking, you should have it too.

SASKI: Do you want me to have it?

NICK: He doesn't want that.

    SASKI studies GEROME.

SASKI: Yes ... you do.

    REID enters with a wine glass and the bottle of wine. MICHAEL follows, grabbing a can of cola from a hiding spot in the cushions of the couch.

REID: I'm telling you, Sueski—

SASKI: Saski—

REID: This kid was so excited to meet you I was worried he was gonna piss himself. Eh, Geromey?

REID hands the glass to SASKI and pours.

SASKI: Oh! That's plenty, thank you!

REID: You're gonna want as much as you can get. You speak any Klingon perchance?

SASKI: Klingon? I do not.

REID: Shucks—woulda helped.

REID points at GEROME.

Don't pee your pants.

REID exits. MARION calls from the kitchen.

MARION: *(off)* THE TATERS ARE ALMOST READY! MICHAEL, WASH UP!

GEROME: I didn't wash my hands for dinner!

NICK: Good thing you didn't forget—

GEROME: I gotta wash my hands.

GEROME exits.

NICK: I feel like I should—ah, I'm sorry.

SASKI: No, no. Glad he told me himself.

NICK: If you're uncomfortable you don't have to stay.

SASKI: He's a lovely young man who happens to be a consumer of the mental-health industry.

NICK: "Consumer"! Yeah, that would suggest there was a customer complaints line and full money-back guarantee—

SASKI grabs her cell.

SASKI: Let me get you the number of the head of psychology at McGill. He and I met in grad school.

NICK: Oh, is he gonna give us all our money back? No, we've got a whole team of medical people for Gerome—

SASKI: For you, Nicholas. He's excellent. In his private practice he deals with all forms of trauma.

NICK: This isn't traumatic.

SASKI: Mmhmm. But who will "care for the carer"?

NICK: Ha!

SASKI holds out her cell with the contact information. NICK shakes his head.

You changed your hair.

SASKI: The neon green wasn't exactly natural. It was a bingo marker.

NICK: It was quick when we met, but I'm having a real hard time recognizing you.

SASKI: That's a huge compliment.

NICK imitates SASKI from when they first met.

NICK: "Are you two gay together?"

SASKI: Please disregard everything I said to you and/or your partner—

NICK: "You fucking rock!"

SASKI: Oh dear. Where is he this weekend?

NICK: Who knows—no, he's back in Montreal. He couldn't—ah—take . . . I dunno. "Who will care for the carer?" Who cares who cares for the carer?

SASKI: In your position, I would need someone to talk to.

NICK: I'm getting all the support I can take. All three of us are—it's great. Toby's probably at his second job right now. Eight to six he's in the office, then he's working evenings, and on his one night off a week he's got a group for parents whose kids have schizophrenia, which doesn't leave him a lot of time with Gerome to apply what he's learning—but we're trying to make sure we all get what we need—and that's what he needs right now. He needs time and space.

SASKI: Nicholas—

NICK: And he shows how much he cares. Every day he puts up these signs—an idea he got from the group—"how to live" reminders all around the apartment. "This is the kitchen where we all eat together." Except not usually.

SASKI: I think you need someone to talk to.

MARION calls from the kitchen.

MARION: *(off)* NICK! COME SCRAPE THE BURNT BITTIES OFF YOUR CASSEROLE!

NICK: *(calling off)* OKAY!

GEROME enters from upstairs.

(to SASKI) Sorry about—all that.

SASKI: No apologies. Gerome, your father was explaining how supportive he is of you. It's wonderful.

NICK: *(to GEROME)* Wanna come save dinner?

GEROME: No.

SASKI: We'll manage.

NICK: Call me if—

GEROME: BYE, PAPA.

NICK exits to the kitchen.

SASKI: I can't believe how much you remind me of your . . . bio father.

GEROME: Where is he?

SASKI: I don't know. He was my boyfriend of a few weeks. We haven't been in touch since I was fifteen.

A slight pause.

Thank you for instigating this. It's a beautiful thing we're here together.

GEROME starts moving his fingers as before.

GEROME: If it's a beautiful thing why are you leaving early?

SASKI: I wanted to see how the night . . . played out. On my way over I was so nervous.

GEROME: Because of me?

SASKI: I was saying, "Think of yourself fifteen years younger, and a boy." But you're nothing like me. When I was seventeen, you were two years old and I would imagine you and I were—might be—connected. That I could sense what you were thinking. Feeling. Did you ever—

NICK's cellphone rings.

Do you need to get that?

GEROME takes it out of his pocket and silences it. He does his gesture over the phone to make it safe. GEROME starts whispering to himself.

Gerome?

MICHAEL pulls off his headphones.

MICHAEL: He's hearing his voices.

SASKI: *(to GEROME)* How do I help? . . . Let them out.

GEROME: You won't like it—

SASKI: Are they speaking about me?

GEROME starts quickly tapping his temples with his fingers over and over, growing almost violent.

Hold on—you don't have to say. I already know.

GEROME stops and looks at her.

I can hear them too.

MICHAEL: You can?

SASKI: They're calling me names—

GEROME covers his ears.

GEROME: No, shhh—

SASKI: They think I'm going to run away, is that it?

MARION enters from the kitchen with oven mitts on and a casserole dish.

MARION: Watch out, everyone, this is piping hot—

GEROME: *(to MARION)* I'm sorry—

GEROME grabs for the dish with both hands.

MARION: No!

MARION tries to pull the dish away, but it's too late.

SASKI: GEROME!

GEROME lets go of the dish.

GEROME: FUCK!

NICK enters from the kitchen, running.

MARION: Your hands!

NICK: What happened?

GEROME: I needed a better distraction.

NICK: *(to SASKI)* Were you watching him at all?

SASKI: I didn't—

MARION: It was my fault—

NICK: Let's get them under cold water.

NICK leads GEROME out. MARION puts down the dish and exits after them.

SASKI: *(calling off)* Can I do something?

MARION: *(off)* MICHAEL, SHOW SASKI SOME PARADISE!

SASKI: Paradise?

MICHAEL: Lost. School play. It's pretty shitty.

SASKI: *"Sing Muse—"*

MICHAEL: I'm not doing any for you. If you're lucky I'll show you my costume later. How do you know what his voices are saying?

SASKI: I guessed.

MICHAEL considers this, then nods.

MICHAEL: I'll bet you thirty bucks I can do five backflips in a row. Deal?

SASKI: Ahhhhhhh—

REID enters with a wine glass.

REID: He can kiss his life as a hand supermodel goodbye—that kid's gonna be marked for years.

SASKI: No!

REID: I'm kidding—

MARION enters from the kitchen.

MARION: *(to MICHAEL)* Did you wash your hands?

MICHAEL: Saski wants to see my backflips.

REID snaps at him and gestures for him to go. MICHAEL exits upstairs.

SASKI: How's Gerome?

MARION: Don't worry, his papa's got him. I was just saying to everyone in there how much I like you—

MARION gives SASKI a big hug.

You walked in and Geromey looked you up and down when he thought you weren't looking—it was the cutest ever.

SASKI: I hope I satisfy.

MARION: Oh, you more than do. But seriously, you two look like you were separated at birth. I mean, I know you were, but you look like long-lost twins! You could be seventeen! Let's see some ID, young lady, before you have a second glass—

SASKI: I'm thirty-two.

MARION: Well, I want what you're drinking cuz I feel like I could be your mother.

SASKI: I think we're the same age, aren't we?

MARION: Oh! You're a keeper!

Loud thumping can be heard from above.

(calling off) NO ACROBATICS IN THE HOUSE, MICHAEL!

MICHAEL: *(off)* THAT WAS FIVE BACKFLIPS IN A ROW! SASKI OWES ME THIRTY BUCKS!

MARION shakes her head pleasantly at SASKI.

MARION: Are you from the Bay originally?

SASKI: I grew up here.

MARION: Us too! Born and raised! What's your high school?

SASKI: St. Ignatius—

MARION: Oh my goodness—go Falcons go! Reid!

REID: Yeah?

MARION: She's a Falconer too!

REID takes a big sip of wine.

REID: I heard!

MARION: Saint I reunion!

(re: NICK and REID) Those two are a pair of golden oldies—before our time—but what if you and me were there together and I was a senior and you were in grade nine—oh my goodness I could have been your peer buddy for first week and showed you around and tutored you on homework and after we'd talk about your problems and boys and I could have given you advice and maybe we could have even been friends and stayed in touch till right now.

SASKI: Maybe.

MARION: When did you graduate?

SASKI: Ten years ago. I took extra time.

MARION: And now look at you. Dr. Halton!

SASKI: I have a Ph.D. I'm not a medical—

MARION: Doesn't even matter, it's so inspiring. You should write.

SASKI: I do.

MARION: You should write your story because it is fantastic and I would read it! Do you have children?

REID downs the rest of his wine.

REID: Excluding the kid in the next room, of course.

SASKI: No. And I don't want any.

REID exits to the kitchen without MARION noticing.

MARION: Mmmm, really? We would chew glass—

MARION looks for REID and realizes he's gone. She starts again.

I would chew glass to have a baby.

SASKI: Michael isn't yours?

MARION shakes her head.

MARION: But maybe I should just try writing like you, huh?

NICK and GEROME enter from the kitchen. GEROME is holding a bag of frozen vegetables for the burn.

You should write you and Gerome's story!

SASKI: We don't have much of a story. Yet.

MARION: *(to GEROME)* Would you like that?

MARION examines his hands.

Ohhhhh!

NICK: He's fine, Marion—

MARION: *(announcing)* Yep—he's gonna be fine! Okay, Geromey, I want you right here beside your mom, and I'll be on the other side of her—and I don't care about the rest of you, you sit where you want. No, I'm joking—Nick, you there—

(calling off) REID! MICHAEL! COME ON!

REID enters with the bottle of wine NICK brought.

REID: Onto number two. Can we get you some wine, babe?

MARION: One little splash for the special occasion.

MICHAEL enters from upstairs.

SASKI: *(to GEROME)* I almost forgot—an early birthday card—or a belated one if we agree that it will strike the last seventeen missed birthdays from the record.

GEROME is still holding the frozen veggies. SASKI opens the card for him. A cheque falls out.

MICHAEL picks up the cheque.

MICHAEL: This is for five trillion dollars!

MARION: MICHAEL!

SASKI takes the cheque and gives it to GEROME.

SASKI: I wish.

NICK: You're giving him money?

SASKI: I thought it could be for post-secondary education.

NICK: *(to GEROME)* Can I see that?

SASKI: It's Gerome's.

NICK: Excuse me?

SASKI: *(to GEROME)* What schools are you thinking? Put Lakehead in the running.

NICK: We're focusing on getting his high school diploma. We'd be thrilled with that given . . . everything we're dealing with.

MARION gestures to SASKI and tries to mouth the words "does she know?" to NICK.

Yes, she knows.

SASKI: *(to GEROME)* Be future-oriented. Lakehead's cognitive science research program. If you're fascinated by the brain. It's up and coming.

NICK: I can't see him in a dorm.

SASKI: I have a spare room.

NICK: Whoa!

MARION: That's generous—

SASKI: *(to GEROME)* I mean, if you're interested in coming down on a weekend. Touring the campus. Stay a night.

NICK: Montreal has three internationally known universities. If and when he goes, he's gonna stick closer to home. We can't accept any money.

SASKI: It's not for you.

NICK: Ah, thank you—really very kind—but no.

(to GEROME) Give it back.

GEROME: It's mine.

MICHAEL holds up the card and cheque, moving away from the table.

MICHAEL: Now it's mine!

GEROME: Don't!

MARION: MICHAEL!

MICHAEL reads the card.

MICHAEL: "Dear Gerome, you've had my love longer than you've been in the world—"

REID grabs him by the arm and takes the card.

REID: Sit! Behave!

MICHAEL: Ow! Fuck off.

REID flicks MICHAEL in the ear.

MARION: Watch the L-A-N-A-G-U . . . E.

SASKI: *(to REID)* What was that?

REID: It was a flick.

MICHAEL: "Lana-goooo"?

MARION: You know what I mean—

SASKI: *(to REID)* Because he said "fuck off"?

MARION: *(to SASKI)* We actually don't support language like that.

MICHAEL: *(to MARION)* You're such a 'tard.

REID: See, he's not really fazed, is he?

SASKI: Try flicking my ear.

REID: Oh, come on, he can do it to me—Mikey, flick!

NICK: Let it go, Reid.

REID: *(to MICHAEL)* Come on, fucking flick me!

MARION: Fuck fuck fuck! Let's all forget our manners!

MICHAEL flicks MARION. REID can't help but laugh.

MICHAEL!

SASKI flicks REID.

REID: Ah! Lightly! You wailed me—I'm wounded.

SASKI: Ha! Oh please!

NICK: Everyone needs to cool it.

MARION: Yes, everyone needs to think meditation!

REID: *(to GEROME)* My man, flick Michael, it'll make you feel better.

NICK: No—

REID *flicks* NICK. GEROME *laughs.*

Ow, jackass!

MICHAEL: *(chanting)* Fight! Fight! Fight! Fight!

GEROME: *(joining in)* Fight! Fight! Fiiiight fiiiight iiiight iiiii ...

GEROME's *chanting turns into a moan.* MICHAEL *covers his ears.* GEROME *continues through the following, growing steadily quieter.*

MARION: No yelling at the dinner table, please!

MICHAEL: Why is he making those sounds?

NICK: *(to REID)* Thank you for this—

REID: What did I do?

SASKI *is on her cell and plays Hans Rott's Symphony in E major.* GEROME *becomes silent.* SASKI *closes her eyes, sways for a few moments, and sighs.*

SASKI: Do you recognize this?

MARION: No.

SASKI: Gerome? We listened to it together. Before you were in the world ... earphones on my belly ...

(to NICK) Do you mind me talking about this?

NICK shakes his head.

(to GEROME) It was soothing—and it meant a smart baby. That's what they said.

SASKI gestures to GEROME.

Proof.

MARION: Aw! This night deserves a toast! I'M MAKING A SPEECH!

REID: Oh please god—mercy, mercy.

MARION ignores him.

MARION: I go to Toastmasters and they're all about saying only what you've got to say and planning it out and tonight is the night. Reunion, mother and son. We need to mark it. So I'm thinking, "I better write something"—and I am at the kitchen table, scratching away, making a list of your names, and then it hits me. "Okay, Marion—but! What if you can't find the words to say it?" Cuz this weekend has taught me that if you try and try and try so hard to show that you're good at something, you'll get given that something. Gerome, he's the perfect example. He's trying so hard to be okay and he's okay—he is! And I'm trying so hard and I-I-I get all of you as gifts—and I'm gonna keep trying and maybe ... um ... I ...

MARION starts fanning her face.

Oh, sorry–

REID takes her hand and raises his glass.

REID: To pineapple, baby.

MICHAEL: What the frick?

MARION raises a glass.

MARION: To fertile pineapple! Now—

(re: food) Who wants more? No one better be full! Gerome! I know you have a big appetite!

GEROME is mumbling to himself and covers his ears. MARION reaches out to touch him and GEROME screams in her face and draws back suddenly.

I didn't touch him!

GEROME: No, I said no!

(mumbling) Cut out my shoulder blades, that'd be okay, I'll use them for wings—

REID: Yeeeeah, so meditation's sounding pretty good—how do we do that?

NICK tries to make eye contact with GEROME.

NICK: Gerome, eyes—here—where are your eyes?

GEROME points at MARION.

GEROME: She wants to cut me open but my bones are wings—I'll get away!

SASKI: Listen to me, Gerome. I was sent. By the voices.

NICK: What's going on?

SASKI: To help you.

NICK: You're facilitating delusional thinking—

SASKI points at MARION.

SASKI: She won't hurt us.

GEROME covers his ears and mumbles to himself unintelligibly.

NICK: *(to SASKI)* Did it work?

REID: Anyone know psycho first aid?

NICK puts himself beside GEROME, not directly in front of him.

NICK: Bud, what do we have to remember about the voices?

GEROME shakes his head, distracted.

They're in your head.

GEROME: They're too loud.

NICK: If they're only in your head, who's stronger?

GEROME: What if . . .

GEROME trails off, distracted again.

NICK: What if what?

GEROME: They're not in my head?

NICK: That's possible too. I'm not saying it isn't—

GEROME suddenly and quickly moves to go.

Sit, stay. Don't do what the voices tell you—

GEROME points at MARION.

GEROME: I don't want her here—

REID: She can go—

NICK: She's not going anywhere. You are stronger than anything in your head.

MARION holds up her hands.

MARION: My hands are empty and—

MARION puts her hands over her eyes.

My eyes aren't gonna kill you either.

MICHAEL plays "Mama Said" on the iPad again.

REID: Mike—

MICHAEL: He likes it—

MARION's up and bouncing to the music with her hands over her eyes.

MARION: It'll distract him! Gerome! Show us your moves!

MICHAEL and MARION both sing along.

NICK: Look at me. This is you putting up a fight.

GEROME nods, but he's still distracted.

MARION starts clapping.

MARION: Yay! Our beautiful nephew's back!

GEROME starts singing along quietly to the song.

NICK hands SASKI the birthday card.

NICK: *(to SASKI, quietly)* Might be almost eight.

SASKI: *(to NICK, mostly)* Oops. Is that the time already?

SASKI puts GEROME's card on the table as NICK grabs the iPad and turns down the music.

NICK: Gerome! You wanna say goodbye to Saski?

GEROME: *(to SASKI)* Why did it matter if I was smart?

SASKI: Of course it mattered.

GEROME: But why would it matter to you?

SASKI: Whether or not I was giving up the baby—

GEROME: Me—

NICK: Don't let feelings sneak up on you, bud.

SASKI: You. Whether or not I was giving you up. I needed to know there was a person out there I consciously contributed to.

GEROME: My ventricles are enlarged.

SASKI: I don't know what—

GEROME: They're the spaces inside heads—more ventricles, more emptiness—less brain. Your—

He imitates Rott's Symphony in E major.

Didn't help with that. Schizophrenia is all wide-open spaces.

SASKI: I don't think they know where schizophrenia comes from.

GEROME knocks on his skull.

GEROME: I know what comes from you.

NICK: Emotional regulation, let's do the steps. One: name the emotion—

GEROME: I don't feel emotion, I'm a Vulcan—

He waves SASKI away.

"LIVE LONG AND PROSPER!" We're talking about diminished cognitions!

NICK: *(to GEROME)* You have to cool it.

SASKI: *(to GEROME)* "Diminished cognitions"?

NICK: *(to SASKI)* It's probably best if you—

MARION: No, come on—just change the subject. Black holes! Geromey and Michael know all about black holes!

SASKI: *(to GEROME)* You seem extremely intelligent to me.

GEROME: When exactly were you going to check up on my brainpower?

NICK: *(to SASKI)* Ignore that question.

SASKI: No, it's valuable. Gerome. I wasn't around because . . . my presence in your life . . . was not encouraged.

NICK: What is that supposed to mean?

REID: Oh-ho, take it like a bitch, Nickster.

MARION: REID!

GEROME: *(to SASKI)* But it's up to you, right?

SASKI: It's up to everybody. All the adults. My having contact with you . . . was not fostered.

REID's cellphone rings.

NICK: We didn't stop you from knowing him—

REID answers his cell.

REID: *(to cell)* Reid here. Go.

SASKI: We have different perspectives.

REID: *(to cell)* Toby, my man! How's all that work treating ya?

NICK: There are no perspectives!

MARION: Emotions! Emotions!

REID: *(to NICK)* Preach it!

(to cell) . . . Oh, he isn't answering, huh?

NICK: You were fifteen. You said—

SASKI: Right, yes! Fifteen! Of course I said something stupid!

REID: *(to cell)* . . . Yeah, he's too busy ripping into the woman who bore your child.

NICK: No, you said to us—

REID: Yo, Nicky—

NICK: And the social worker—

MARION: RED ALERT!

REID: Hubby wants to know—

NICK: And all the doctors and the nurses—

REID: Did you fix Gerome?

NICK: I—NO!

MARION: PERSIANS! How about we all have Persians!

NICK: You said to anyone who would fucking listen if you never—

> *MARION lets out a scream and throws some broccoli at NICK. She misses and hits REID.*

MARION: *(to NICK)* Don't you dare, don't you dare!

> *REID throws the broccoli back at her.*

REID: Don't YOU dare!

REID follows it up with a volley of tater tots—a direct hit, and MARION screams.

MARION: You got me in the eye!

REID: No I didn't!

MICHAEL throws broccoli at her and misses. MARION exits to the kitchen. REID throws food at his son.

(to MICHAEL) Hey, what are you fucking doing? Behave yourself.

(to cell) . . . You getting all this, Toby?

NICK: Gimme the phone!

NICK grabs the phone from his brother and exits to the kitchen.

(to cell) Toby—?

REID and MICHAEL are firing food back and forth across the room at each other. SASKI takes cover and GEROME is now seated at the table and doesn't seem to notice.

GEROME: What did you say to everyone when I was born?

SASKI shakes her head.

SASKI: I have no idea. I was too busy giving birth.

GEROME gets up.

GEROME: May I be excused?

SASKI: Where are you going?

REID: Go for it—

SASKI: But where—

GEROME exits and MICHAEL follows.

REID: *(calling after him)* Mikey! Leave the poor kid alone!

MARION enters with a can of beer eating a Persian. She opens her beer.

Truce and cheers, babe?

REID reaches for the Persian, but MARION doesn't let him.

SASKI: Nicholas is a passionate father.

MARION: No better papa than Nick.

SASKI: Is that true? No better father?

REID: Ahhhh—yeah.

SASKI: At least you're protective of each other. But you're family? Not the most objective. It's the hardest thing. To say "I don't think so and so is such a . . . "

SASKI trails off.

MARION: Is that what you're saying? Wait—such a what?

MICHAEL enters.

SASKI: It's terrifying to be called out on. And this is a faux pas. As a non-parent. Me. Talking about his parenting. Not allowed.

MARION: No, not in front of the K-I-D-S! Michael, where's Gerome?

MICHAEL: Get ready.

MARION: *(calling off)* GEROMEY, EAT YOUR PERSIANS!

> *GEROME enters. He is shirtless and his torso is clean of writing. He offers SASKI the permanent marker.*

REID: Booyah! This party's gettin' naked!

GEROME: Sign.

MARION: This isn't marker time. I want that shirt on. Dessert, everyone!

MICHAEL: Ewwww, I'm not having floor dessert!

GEROME: *(to SASKI)* Sign your name. SIGN IT!

> *MICHAEL grabs the pen and tries to sign his name. GEROME lunges and screams at him.*

MARION: STOP!

> *REID steps in front of GEROME.*

REID: *(to GEROME)* Back off.

(to MICHAEL) Go to your room.

> *MICHAEL doesn't leave. GEROME lies down on the ground.*

GEROME: I need proof you're my mother.

MARION: Oh, she is, honey—she is, she is, she is!

GEROME covers his ears.

GEROME: Ahhhh!

(to SASKI) You're looking at me like the rest of them, thinking, "Oh oh oh, if only he could help himself."

SASKI: Not at all.

GEROME: Hold on to your quiet, ordinary thoughts a little more tightly, babe: your brain is plaid, it's saran wrap. And I hear angels. They talk to me—they chose me—

(to SASKI) Can't you hear them?

SASKI shakes her head.

You lied.

SASKI: I thought I could understand.

REID puts up his hand.

REID: Actually, the angels chose me.

MARION: Reid!

REID: This is what Nicky did. You gotta reason him out of it—

(to GEROME) I'm the chosen one.

GEROME: No, I am—

REID: We can't both be the chosen one.

GEROME's lips are moving, and he writes a "G" on his face in a big messy block letter.

Never mind, you're the chosen one.

GEROME writes "E" and "R" on his chest.

MARION: My turn for the pen!

GEROME writes the "O" over his belly button. To continue writing his name, he starts to take off his pants.

SASKI: All right, I'll sign!

SASKI holds out her hand. GEROME doesn't give her the marker.

GEROME: Too late. You were supposed to be like me.

NICK enters. GEROME drops the marker.

I want to go home.

NICK looks tired, and his heaviness is palpable. He takes off his suit jacket and puts it over GEROME.

NICK: It's a nineteen-hour drive. A deer smashed our car. We can't go home tonight.

GEROME takes NICK's cellphone out of his pocket and does his gesture to make it safe over and over.

Gimme my phone, Gerome.

GEROME does not respond.

Fine, keep it, I don't care.

SASKI: He's saying the voices are angels—

GEROME: *(re: SASKI)* How is she getting my thoughts?

SASKI: I can't read your thoughts. You told me—

NICK puts his head in his hands.

GEROME: *(to SASKI)* My thoughts are being sent like text messages—you are receiving them. I don't know how you do it, but you do—betraying my thoughts to Serotonin and his legion of archaliens, alien–arches, ARCH ARCH ARCH—

GEROME's voice goes soft abruptly, and he continues under his breath. NICK slumps down to the floor, defeated.

MARION: Not a good time to sit down.

NICK doesn't move.

MICHAEL: Maybe he should take his pills.

MARION: Michael, clear the plates.

MICHAEL: You told me to go to my room.

MARION: Then go to your room!

MICHAEL: But—

REID: GO!

MICHAEL exits.

GEROME: I'm breaking open—there's only smooth *craten* edges, no cracks—as if I was always *grunden,* meant to be in pieces from the start.

REID: What the fuck's *"grunden"*? Klingon?

MARION: It doesn't mean anything in Klingon—he's making up words.

REID: Oh, we're on to gibberish—greaaaat. Everyone know where the emergency exits are?

SASKI: Is it necessary to joke?

GEROME: You are all traitors—

MARION: We're keeping you safe—

GEROME starts dialing a number on the cell.

GEROME: LET ME GO HOME!

MARION: Is it time to call the hospital yet?

GEROME: *(to cell)* Hello?

(a wail) Daaaaaaaad!

NICK: *(quietly)* Fuck!

(to GEROME) Give me the phone—

NICK shouts into the cell.

TOBY, IT'S UNDER CONTROL!

GEROME: You have to come pick me up right now! Please!

NICK grabs GEROME.

NICK: He's hours away!

GEROME throws the cell at NICK, and NICK ducks.

MARION: GEROME!

But GEROME is looking past NICK. MICHAEL has entered dressed in his costume for the school play. It's hastily made but hauntingly grotesque, and it engulfs him. Makeup covers his face.

MICHAEL: This is my costume!

GEROME screams, unable to look away, terrified.

REID: Fuck off!

MICHAEL: He'll like this!

GEROME: STAY AWAY FROM ME!

NICK: Listen to my voice—

MICHAEL: Gerome, it's me!

REID gestures upstairs.

REID: *(to MICHAEL)* GO!

GEROME: DON'T YOU TOUCH ME! YOU GET AWAY FROM ME!

NICK: Focus here—eyes!

GEROME covers his eyes.

GEROME: Getoutofinsideme getoutofinsideme getout getoutout—

MICHAEL: But he knows me.

REID grabs at the costume, and it tears as MICHAEL runs from him. GEROME screams and pounds the floor with his fists. REID chases MICHAEL out.

GEROME: This is the prayer: You live like them for a day—one day singular. Then you're eaten alive, punctured from your sole toooo your eyeball. Keep keep keep yourself like them. I say YES! DEAL! TRADE. All this for one day.

GEROME is curled on the floor, hugging himself. MICHAEL creeps back in with half his costume off, watching. No one notices him.

REID is very shaken by GEROME.

REID: There he is, ladies and gentlemen ... Our fuckin' chosen one!

NICK: No! You don't get to do that right now!

REID tries to laugh.

REID: I know, I know—what the hell's the matter with me?

NICK: Please. Leave.

REID nods.

REID: Yeah, I should um—let's give him some space ... Why do I always have to say shit? I dunno.

REID exits to the kitchen. GEROME is still.

SASKI: I can go too.

NICK: I need his pills.

MARION: What?

NICK crosses to exit upstairs.

NICK: His pills!

MARION: What do we do?

NICK: Keep him there!

NICK exits upstairs. SASKI approaches GEROME and kneels by him.

SASKI: . . . When I was pregnant, your father, he left these home-made VHS recordings, *Star Trek: The Next Generation* episodes by the boxful. I watched them with you religiously. You kicked whenever the theme music came on. He was an interesting . . . boy, your daddy. He had visions of the future. He said he saw himself on a starship in his mind, exploring beyond the known universe. And I wonder if . . .

SASKI's hand hovers above GEROME for a moment and then she stands. She goes to gather her things.

I have to—I'm already late—

MARION: Ah—sorry, where?

SASKI: I can't offer anything that matters.

MARION: No, but—where is more important than here?

SASKI: He wouldn't like me to see this.

SASKI goes to exit. MICHAEL takes GEROME's pill bottle from his pocket. MICHAEL goes to GEROME and puts the pill bottle in his hand. GEROME exits with the bottle. SASKI and MARION don't see any of this. SASKI is outside the house and turns back to MARION, standing at the door.

When he comes back to you. Tell him I left earlier.

MARION: He wanted proof you were his mother.

SASKI: This is a . . . family-only time.

SASKI exits. Faintly, the sound of GEROME shaking the pill bottle, as he did in scene two, can be heard—almost an echo of the original sound. MARION turns and notices GEROME is gone.

MARION: Where—?

MICHAEL: I had them. I gave them to him.

MARION: You—?

MICHAEL: His pills.

NICK's cell starts ringing from where GEROME left it on the floor.

MARION: *(calling off)* GEROME?

MICHAEL picks it up and answers it.

MICHAEL: *(to cell)* Hi, Uncle Toby.

GEROME enters.

Yeah, Gerome's here.

MICHAEL holds out the cell but keeps his distance.

(to GEROME) It's for you.

MARION takes the cell from MICHAEL and goes to hand it to GEROME. The empty pill bottle and cap drop from GEROME's hands. He's shaking his head furiously.

GEROME: I need to—

MICHAEL: Did you take them all?

MARION: No— Oh—

(to cell) Toby, I need help—he's—

GEROME sticks his hand down his throat, trying to make himself vomit.

Oh my god!

MARION drops the phone and grabs GEROME but doesn't know what to do. NICK enters running.

NICK: It's okay, you're okay, shhh—what happened?

MARION: No no no no no!

MICHAEL: Why would you take them all?

MARION finds her voice.

MARION: Get in the car! Get him in the car!

NICK: He's gonna be fine, you're fine—

MARION: No, we have to go—

(calling off) Reid!

MICHAEL holds up the empty pill bottle.

MICHAEL: What if he takes them all?

NICK realizes what his son has done.

NICK: I'm so stupid, I'm so—you have to be fine, please be fine!

REID enters from the kitchen.

MARION: Stay with Michael!

MICHAEL: Gerome!

REID holds his son. MARION and NICK support GEROME out. NICK's cell begins to ring again from its place on the floor. Lights out.

SCENE SEVEN

REID is setting up a tent in the living room. It's late the following afternoon. It looks like he hasn't slept, and he's got a small, fresh bandage on his nose. NICK, GEROME, and MARION enter. They haven't slept either. GEROME is moving his fingers in a repetitive motion as before, but the quality is different now—the movement is softer. NICK is almost hysterical with exhaustion.

NICK: What's this?

REID: You two were supposed to camp.

MARION gently inspects REID's nose.

NICK: Toby's flying out right now for Gerome. I'll wait for the shop to fix his car and drive back tomorrow by myself.

REID: So have breakfast in it.

NICK sits.

NICK: It's four in the afternoon.

REID: Serve it all day in this house.

NICK: *(re: GEROME)* He can't eat and I don't want to.

REID: Gotta eat.

MARION yawns.

MARION: I'll make eggs.

MARION exits to the kitchen.

REID: *(to NICK)* How many—

But NICK has fallen asleep sitting up. REID covers him with a blanket. GEROME whispers to himself—just briefly—and REID doesn't hear him. REID moves to exit.

GEROME: Uncle Reid?

REID: Uh-huh?

GEROME: They had to perform a gastric lavage.

REID: I heard. I usually call it getting your stomach pumped, but okay.

GEROME: I passed out thinking about what you said—

REID: Take what I say with any authority and it will fuck you up.

GEROME: But about being a shaman—

REID: Especially that.

GEROME: The voices might be beautiful but—

REID: They aren't! You are way smarter than me. Why the fuck would you listen?

GEROME: I don't want to be a shaman. And I don't think I believe in the voices.

MARION enters from the kitchen.

REID: Ha—fucking seventeen-year-old, huh? Stays up all night getting his belly emptied—he looks great. The rest of us look four hundred years old.

REID exits to the kitchen.

MARION: *(calling off)* MICHAEL, HOW MANY EGGS?

MICHAEL enters in GEROME's original jacket and tie. The tie is stuck back together with tape and wrapped around his forehead like a bandana.

MICHAEL: I wanna make 'em.

MARION: Go help your father.

MICHAEL: *(to GEROME)* Hey.

GEROME: Hi.

MICHAEL hugs GEROME.

MICHAEL: *(re: tie)* Can I keep this?

GEROME nods. REID enters with the empty wine bottles and beer cans. MARION takes them.

MARION: It's really not that bad. We were modest—don't you think? . . . I'll put them outside.

MICHAEL opens the front door for MARION and helps with the empties. They exit outside.

REID: NICKY!

NICK jumps awake.

Eggs! How many? . . . We'll make you three—winners eat three.

REID exits.

GEROME: Papa?

NICK: Uh-huh?

GEROME: Maybe they're the crazy ones.

NICK laughs, and his laugh goes on. Pause. GEROME closes his eyes and whispers to himself, but it has a kind quality, gentle and comforting.

NICK: How are you feeling? Voices?

GEROME: The usual chatter. But the volume's low—really low. Papa, we don't have to tell Dad I skipped pills.

NICK: You trying to protect me? I called him when you were passed out. He knows. There's a long-lasting medication that they can inject—it'll go for a couple of weeks, then you go back for a top-up and—it's ongoing maintenance. Best we can do right now. Dad's gonna talk to you about it.

GEROME: Is that what you want for me?

NICK: It doesn't matter what—yes. I want to keep you solid.

GEROME: First you want me off the medication—

NICK: I was wrong—

GEROME: Yeah, but I wanted off the medication too—

NICK: I know—

GEROME: And now you want me to shoot it up?

NICK: I don't know what the answer is!

GEROME: I don't know either, but Dad's right. You're all or nothing.

I think you want me to say no to the shots. I think you want me to say I'll be stronger.

NICK: If I could figure out how to bring you back from that darkness you have to visit, I would.

But your body. We have to work with your body. And your mind . . . Focus on what's possible . . . Gerome. I'm so exhausted.

GEROME: Go back to sleep.

NICK: No, no—please, listen. Dad's also going to talk to you about, um—other arrangements for . . . group homes or supportive living—

GEROME: Why?

NICK: I can't—I am obviously not capable of caring for you—

GEROME: I don't want you to. I don't want Dad to either—

NICK: Yeah, you're gonna be an adult—you are an adult. You deserve independence—a group home is close. Cuz you still need someone. Other than me, by myself. I . . . did this.

GEROME: But we were being defiant.

NICK: Sweetie—

GEROME: I'll think about the shots. I'll think about the group home. My choices. Right?

NICK nods.

I'll still be defiant.

NICK: You have to get that I fucked up. You have to understand that.

GEROME: I can take the drug shots, but imagine it's you bringing me back from the darkness, like we can be camping right now, beside the moon, in outer space. We go swimming, floating from star to star. We come up for air—there is none, but we're breathing. No oxygen required.

GEROME gets in the tent and faces outward. His father gets in the tent beside him.

We can be defiant like that. Together. It doesn't always have to be real.

GEROME has the card from SASKI and he hands it to NICK.

Look inside.

NICK opens the card.

NICK: What's this?

NICK takes out a photo and they hold it together.

It's your ultrasound. That's you.

GEROME: See the resemblance? It looks like I'm in the stars. Breathing outer space.

Lights fade to a starscape spread across the darkness, slowly becoming an ultrasound, and eventually fade to black.

ACKNOWLEDGEMENTS

I want to thank every single person who offered their artistry and support to *Quick Bright Things*:

Del Surjik, thank you for your vision that embraced the stars, the laughter, and all of the possibilities in this play, including its final image. Johnna Wright, for your unwavering belief in a script that you plucked from a cold submission email.

Christine Quintana and Laura McLean, thank you for believing in this play when it was only a ten-page infant and for tirelessly supporting its development into a fully grown script.

To my mom, Kathleen MacLeod, for bringing home a computer so I could try writing a sci-fi novel at the age of thirteen.

I'm honoured to write characters that speak to different mental health experiences. Thank you to all the folks at Playwrights Canada Press for championing this story.

I am grateful to live and create on the traditional unceded territories of the xʷməθkwəy̓əm (Musqueam), Skwxwú7mesh (Squamish), and Səl̓ílwətaʔ/Selilwitulh (Tsleil-Waututh) nations, where I wrote this work.

Christopher Cook is a queer theatre artist and therapist living, creating, and playing in Vancouver. His writing credits include *The Better Parts of Mourning, Strip, Gerty—Live! In Concert!*, and *Quick Bright Things*. As a therapist, he specializes in counselling members of the queer and trans communities. As a clinician–researcher, his research focuses on exploring the therapeutic significance of artmaking and creativity. Whether through therapy or theatre, his goal is to engage your head, heart, and body.

First edition: April 2020
Printed and bound in Canada by Rapido Books, Montreal

Jacket photo © Standret | Dreamstime.com
Author photo © Matt Reznek

202-269 Richmond St. W.
Toronto, ON
M5V 1X1

416.703.0013
info@playwrightscanada.com
www.playwrightscanada.com
@playcanpress